THE INSIDER'S GUIDE TO INDEPENDENT FILM DISTRIBUTION

THE INSIDER'S GUIDE TO INDEPENDENT FILM DISTRIBUTION

Stacey Parks

ELSEVIER

AMSTERDAM • BOSTON • HEIDELBERG • LONDON
NEW YORK • OXFORD • PARIS • SAN DIEGO
SAN FRANCISCO • SINGAPORE • SYDNEY • TOKYO
Focal Press is an imprint of Elsevier

Focal Press

Publisher: Elinor Actipis
Publishing Services Manager: George Morrison
Senior Project Manager: Brandy Lilly
Associate Editor: Cara Anderson
Assistant Editor: Robin Weston
Marketing Manager: Christine Degon Veroulis
Interior Design: Dennis Schaefer

Focal Press is an imprint of Elsevier
30 Corporate Drive, Suite 400, Burlington, MA 01803, USA
Linacre House, Jordan Hill, Oxford OX2 8DP, UK

∞ Recognizing the importance of preserving what has been written, Elsevier prints its books
on acid-free paper whenever possible.

Library of Congress Cataloging-in-Publication Data
Parks, Stacey.
    The insider's guide to independent film distribution / Stacey Parks.
      p. cm.
    Includes index.
    ISBN-13: 978-0-240-80922-9 (pbk. : alk. paper)
    ISBN-10: 0-240-80922-X (pbk. : alk. paper)   1. Motion pictures—Marketing.
  2. Motion pictures—Distribution.   3. Motion pictures—Production and direction.
  I. Title.
  PN1995.9.M29P37 2007
  384'.84—dc22

                                    2006102577

British Library Cataloguing-in-Publication Data
A catalogue record for this book is available from the British Library.

ISBN: 978-0-240-80922-9

For information on all Focal Press publications
visit our website at www.books.elsevier.com

07 08 09 10 11 5 4 3 2 1

Printed in the United States of America

Contents

7 After the Distribution Deal 107

8 Self-Distribution and Other Alternatives to Traditional Distribution 115

Appendix A: Anatomy of a Distribution Agreement 141

Appendix B: Sample U.S. Distribution Contract 149

Introduction

If you've been an aspiring filmmaker or just a film fan for the past few years, then you already know how rapidly the world of film distribution is changing.

Take television, for instance. Not only are there new movie channels being added every month to conventional cable platforms, but there are new platforms—such as digital cable and pay-per-view—that have hundreds of unique channels unto themselves. Add to that services such as TiVo and Netflix, and, well, it's obvious the demand for watching movies at home has been increasing at a steady pace.

The Internet is another example. Just a few years ago, we were all on dial-up connections. Today, with broadband connections spreading like wildfire, we can now download movies to our computer and watch them there or on our TV.

Unfortunately for the filmmaker, although the demand for movies continues to rise, the supply of movies on the market continues to rise as well. Innovation in technology over the past five years means that almost anyone can make an independent film these days. Barriers to entry have been eliminated. Although this may be good news for aspiring filmmakers, the other side of the coin is that the oversupply of independent films on the market has caused acquisition prices paid by theatrical distributors, broadcast networks, and DVD companies to dramatically decrease. Where buyers once paid hundreds of thousands of dollars to license an independent film, they now pay less than a hundred thousand dollars. As a result, producers and investors rarely recover their initial investment in the films they make.

However, do not get discouraged. The other reason that fewer and fewer independent films are getting distribution is because most filmmakers do not consider the marketability of their film in advance. Fortunately, for this there is a solution. You can certainly take the time to learn about the realities of the market in advance, and then proceed accordingly.

In this book, I will offer you advice that could significantly improve the chances of getting your film distributed. I will offer proven advice on how to make a film that has a chance at distribution, and then I will present you with different options for realistic distribution outlets. Along the way, we will look at some success stories and hear directly from buyers what they are seeking. Stephen Winter, producer of Jonathan Caouette's *Tarnation*, tells the story of bringing that film to a worldwide audience, as does Betsy Chasse, producer of the successful Samuel Goldwyn theatrical release *What the Bleep Do We Know!?* We'll also hear from Michael Baker—the director of acquisitions at ThinkFilm, home to *Murderball*, Academy Award winner *Born into Brothels*, and Sundance favorite *The Aristocrats*—on the current state of distribution and his advice to filmmakers. We'll hear from several other distributors as well. Finally, several foreign television and DVD buyers will talk about their acquisition guidelines and what they look for in an independent film.

Handbook Overview

Part One looks at the *History of Distribution* and the current *State of the Market,* and why it is so difficult for independent films to find distribution these days. Part One also touches on why acquisition prices are so low in the worldwide marketplace, and discusses the disappearance of distribution advances.

Part Two addresses *Before You Start Production: Getting a Leg Up on Distribution.* It's all about how to research the marketplace before you begin production, which genres and formats are in high demand, how much money you should try to raise, and what your financing options are during this stage.

Part Three covers *Production Geared Toward Distribution,* and is specifically about casting and how to leverage casting into getting distribution for your film. There's an interview with Paul Bales, director of SAGIndie, and how he managed to work with SAG actors on less than a $500K budget. Part Three also covers shooting on digital video versus film, the importance of stills, and writing online production diaries.

Part Four looks at *Postproduction with an Eye Toward Distribution.* Subjects include the importance of M&E (music and effects) tracks, trailers, music clearances, soundtrack albums, and getting objective third-party feedback.

Part Five is called *It's in the Can—Now What?* and is about how to create a campaign for your film; which film festivals to submit to and why; the importance of hiring a PR specialist for a film; the lowdown on producer reps and foreign sales agents, as well as how to find a reputable one; and finally, navigating the international film markets.

Part Six is all about *Getting a Distribution Deal.* It includes the U.S. distribution deal and what to expect, foreign distribution and what to expect, nontheatrical distribution and ancillary markets, and the expenses required to market and distribute your film.

Part Seven subsequently covers *After the Distribution Deal.* This includes realistic sales projections and cash flow for independent films—how much to plan on making and when.

Part Eight is on *Self-Distribution and Other Alternatives to Traditional Distribution.* It introduces do-it-yourself DVD distribution, video on demand, and the platform theatrical release.

Getting your film distributed domestically and/or internationally can open the door to a long and vibrant career as a filmmaker. In fact, it is an essential part in launching your filmmaking career. If they never see your films, an audience will never experience your vision.

If you're going to invest the tremendous time and resources to make a movie, invest wisely and focus on ways that will get your movie distributed—get your movie in front of audiences. By doing this, your career as a successful filmmaker awaits you!

— 1 —

History of Distribution and State of the Market

A Recent History of Distribution

Distribution is the process by which a film reaches the marketplace and is made available to its target audience. Practically speaking, distribution means selling your film to theatrical distributors, broadcast networks, DVD companies, and new-media outlets.

Today it is more difficult than ever to get distribution for your film. Why? Because there are more films on the market than ever before. Historically, it took a lot more effort to make an independent film, and distribution was easier to secure. In the eighties and early nineties, for example, there were a lot fewer independent films in the market, and distributors actually paid advances to secure distribution rights to a film. Because digital technologies hadn't taken hold yet, filmmakers were still shooting their independent films on film, as opposed to digital video. As a result, independent films of the eighties and early nineties tended to be higher quality, and distributors snapped them up at high prices.

Then, in the mid-nineties, the digital revolution began and filmmaking was democratized. Suddenly there were more films on the market than distributors could handle. Filmmakers were thrilled to exercise their artistic license by making films on the new inexpensive format that miniDV delivered. In the process, they flooded the market with independent films. Distributors couldn't keep up.

Acquisition prices started to go down, because as the supply of independent films increased, distributor demand decreased.

By the late nineties, distribution deals became harder and harder to come by. Previously, the pre-sale market had guaranteed distribution in the territory of the presale. Now that market dried up, filmmakers could no longer rely on foreign sales to finance their budgets. Once upon a time, two or three foreign sales could finance an entire independent-film budget, and the rest was profit. By the late nineties and early 2000, that was no longer the case at all. At this point in distribution history, the market turned upside down.

By the years 2001 and 2002, independent films were a commodity. They were sold by the pound to foreign buyers, for a thousand bucks here and there. Now filmmakers had to rely on getting a U.S. distribution deal to recoup their budget. Fortunately, by this point, the U.S. DVD market was hotter than ever. Independent films, especially genre films such as horror or action, were snapped up by U.S. DVD companies to fulfill their output deals with Blockbuster, Hollywood Video, and all the other video stores that were flourishing. Even if the advances these U.S. distributors paid weren't that big, filmmakers were guaranteed royalty checks, which over time helped recoup their budgets and pay back investors.

One downside to this point in distribution history was that although DVD deals were plentiful, it was almost impossible to get a theatrical distribution deal for an independent film. Theater owners just weren't interested in booking the type of independent films that were on the market. Unless the film happened to have a big cast and could guarantee tickets would be sold, or unless the film had just won an audience award at Sundance, advertising prices had gone up so much that the economics simply didn't work anymore. Also, there were so many independent films on the market and not nearly enough screens to put them on. That is one reason why the DVD format became so popular as mass-market distribution.

This brings us to today, where not much has changed in terms of distributor demand and prices paid for independent films, except for one critical development. Fortunately, new-media distribution channels have opened up to absorb some of the supply of films in the market. The Internet, video on demand, and pay-per-view are all distribution channels unique to the past few years that have allowed for greater distribution of independent films. Although these channels do not currently account for big dollars, they are slowly becoming a viable income source for filmmakers. Hopefully, in the next ten years, film budgets will be able to be financed by new-media distribution deals, and will have DVD and theatrical distribution be the profit, turning the market right side up once again.

The Current State of the Market: A Reality Check

A recent survey of domestic and international buyers regarding the state of the market attempted to determine why there has been such a marked price decrease in license fees in the past ten years, as well as a severe drop-off in distribution advances. Here are the survey's findings:

Ten years ago, before every aspiring filmmaker was making a film on a miniDV camera, there were fewer films on the market, and therefore the films that did exist commanded higher licensing fees. Back then, it was even possible to presell certain territories, which meant that a filmmaker would receive money in advance for a project in exchange for the buyer's obtaining exclusive rights to that project in their territory. Therefore, you could essentially raise the money for your movie before shooting it. Unfortunately, those days are gone.

The state of the market is not what it used to be. The truth is that

1. Currently, only the smallest percentage of independent films get U.S. theatrical distribution unless they've won awards at one of the major film festivals or the cast is packed with A-list stars.
2. Once you do start selling your film, it is harder than ever to get companies to agree on paying you the entire license fee up front. Be prepared for payment plans to be spread over long periods of

time. Also know from the outset that there will most likely be long lag times before actual payment reaches you. The reason for this is because DVD companies, for example, receive payments from retailers in increments based on sales of your film. Basically, they don't pay you until they get paid. It's a cash-flow issue.

3. Unfortunately, the days of hefty minimum guarantees (a.k.a. advances) by DVD companies are gone for independent films. Many of the U.S. DVD distributors are currently offering royalty-only deals. This means that you can expect a royalty check about nine months to a year after you sign your distribution deal. This wait is because normally the DVD companies must first recoup their advance and their marketing and manufacturing costs before they pay you royalties. Now, a big part of the reason for the disappearance of advances in the DVD world, I'm told, is due to the fact that you can walk into Wal-Mart and buy big-studio blockbusters for $7.99. So that leaves the $1.99 bin for independent films. Because DVD companies get lower wholesale prices for independent films, they can no longer afford to pay big advances.

Why the Disappearance of Distribution Advances?

In some cases, distributors are willing to take the risk and give a distribution advance to help get the ball rolling or help fill in a financing gap. More often than not, however, distribution advances have caused a number of distributors to go out of business. Some of them started investing insane amounts as production advances or minimum guarantees and were never able to recoup their money. As a result, the rules of the game have been completely rewritten. The new rules are:

1. The production has to have A-list stars attached to the project.
2. The producer has to be innovative and willing to bring other funding to the table.
3. Distributors have to believe the producer can deliver the finished product as promised.

Distributor investments quite often lead to creative collaboration on a project because distributors have been so burned in just giving producers money and waiting for a completed film. On some films, distributors will invest money, then presell whatever territories they can to recoup their advance right away, and in some cases raise additional capital for the film.

The bottom line is that most distributors are reluctant to take the risk in giving an advance. From their point of view, in most cases it just isn't fiscally sound because most projects don't end up making enough sales to cover the advance. And even if they do recoup the advance, it takes several years of sales to get the cash flowing.

So Now What Do You Do?

Despite these discouraging statistics about the market, there are certain types of projects that distributors always seek. Even if you are working with a small budget, there are still both domestic and international distribution possibilities out there.

Although you may not be able to control the dynamics of supply and demand, there are factors you can control—factors that will increase the likelihood of your film's getting distribution. The next chapter will discuss specific steps you can follow.

Interview with U.S. theatrical distributor

Michael Baker, Director of Acquisitions and Development
ThinkFilm (*Shortbus, The Aristocrats, Murderball, Born into Brothels*)

Do you acquire films only at the big film festivals? Or do you also acquire outside of the festivals?
A lot of producers and sales agents have the misconception that your film needs to play in a major festival to have any chance of being bought. It's certainly nice to play Toronto or Sundance or other major festivals, but it's not necessary, and it's not always beneficial. Each festival plays hundreds of films. As a result, it's harder for your film to get any attention or stand

out. There are more films at a festival than any buyer can possibly see. And often a buyer has two or three films playing at the same time, so they are running back and forth between screenings, not seeing each film properly. Or they might really enjoy the first film, so never leave to check out your film. Another situation could occur where you have a decent film that gets overshadowed by other films that happen to be good or simply attract a lot of attention. In each case, the festival hasn't benefited your film.

There is a great opportunity to get your film seen where it will actually receive more attention from the viewer/buyer than at a festival: sending a screener. Many filmmakers are against this. They are proud of their film and believe it needs to be seen on a big screen in a theater to be appreciated properly and assessed at its true value. In reality, acquisitions people are professionals. We screen films via screeners at home or in the office all the time, and we know how to assess things under these circumstances. If we can choose the time when we will watch your film, we'll be more disposed to liking it. As film fans, most of us have great home-entertainment systems—which makes for a better viewing environment than most festival theaters, where other people are running in and out, cell phones are ringing, people are checking email on their Blackberries, and you keep checking your watch because you need to meet someone or get to another screening or get back to the office.

Setting up a private screening in New York or L.A. only inconveniences the buyers more. The last thing we want to do is leave the office in the middle of the day, or give up a free night to go see a movie. Remember, this is work for us. We're looking for an excuse to go home and work on our own scripts.

ThinkFilm has a pretty aggressive acquisition strategy. Does a film still have to have big "names" in order to get a U.S. theatrical release?

Every film needs something to sell it on. A star is a commodity and a sales tool. So anytime you have a "name" in your film, it's going to help. It gives the public a recognizable face, something to reference the film, which is especially important for an independent film, where the marketing budgets tend to be minuscule compared to studio films. A star provides the same safety net for indie pics as it does for studio pictures.

That said, a star is not necessary for a theatrical release. We've bought and released films that have major stars in them, and ones that have only first-time actors. In each case, the film itself was special. Casting a star won't change that.

One problem I encounter regularly is the filmmaker who overestimates the draw of the actor they have cast. There are very few actors who are actually meaningful to the value or release of the film. If someone was the star of a TV series in the eighties, they probably don't mean much. If someone was a direct-to-video star more than five years ago, they probably don't mean much. If someone is going to play a small role in an upcoming theatrical release that has two or three other cast members who are much better known, they probably don't mean much. If someone was on a reality-TV show, they probably don't mean much. It's important to be realistic about the value an actor actually brings to a film.

How many unsolicited screening cassettes do you get a week, and what do you see as the biggest reason to pass on a film?
When it comes down to it, the most common reason we pass on a film is quality, pure and simple. You can have a great concept, or a big budget, or a cool soundtrack, but if the film isn't good, you've got nothing.

Independent film is often review and word-of-mouth driven. We rely on positive reviews and word-of-mouth to fuel knowledge and awareness of our films. We don't have superhero films that are review-proof because they rely on massive marketing campaigns, cool action sequences, and a known franchise or commodity. So if the film doesn't cut it, people won't be encouraged to see it, or they may not even hear about it.

Can a producer expect to recoup his investors' money if he gets a U.S. theatrical deal?
Investing in a film is both risky and lucrative for anyone willing to put money up. Many films don't get picked up or simply don't do well, leaving the investors without any return. When they do pay off, they can pay off very well.

A U.S. theatrical deal for a film is great, because it means there will be tremendous exposure for the film and the opportunity for many people to see it, generating revenues for the film. The other side of this is, a theatrical release is also quite expensive. Prints need to be made, ads booked, publicists hired. Your shipping alone can cost a pretty penny. In most cases, these expenses need to be recouped by the distributor before the producer and his or her investors see any money.

There are certainly examples of independent films that have made money back for their investors while they are in their theatrical release, but it's a safe bet that these films are in the minority.

However, all hope should not be lost. A theatrical release will bring a great deal of attention to the film and likely result in increased revenues from ancillaries, which have much lower expenses. You may be looking at a higher TV sale and better video sales. You may get an airline sale out of it where none was possible before. As a result, there's a good opportunity for the investment to pay off and for your investors to see some money back.

This doesn't mean you should always demand a theatrical release for your film. If it's not appropriate, you will end up spending money to release the film and not get any added value for the ancillaries. Sometimes direct-to-video or a TV premiere is the right financial decision.

As in any business, obviously the amount spent will affect how much money is paid back. If you invest $10 million in a film that gets the same release as a film you invested $2 million in, you'll probably see much more of your money back on the $2 million film.

Do you have any advice for filmmakers who want to make a film that's actually distributable?

Making a film is incredibly exciting. Most filmmakers are very enthusiastic and it is quite inspiring. But enthusiasm is no replacement for skill, research, and preparedness. My advice is not to rush. An idea and a camera are enough to make a film, but not to make a good film. Take your time to develop your script, cast well, get a good camera and test it, rehearse, schedule, do several edits, try and get some more money, secure some name actors, call up any contacts you have for advice and assistance, etc.

Suggested Exercises for Part One

1. Write a paragraph explaining your opinion on the state of the distribution market today and what you would like to see change, if anything.

— 2 —
Before You Start Production: Getting a Leg Up on Distribution

Preproduction is the ideal time to start thinking of distribution for your film. By planning in advance, there are so many things that you can institute at this stage of the game that will give your movie infinitely better chances at distribution later.

In some cases, you can even secure distribution for your film during preproduction. This is called presales. Although presales are very uncommon these days, I know of several indie filmmakers who have managed to presell their projects during preproduction. This way, the movies are guaranteed distribution when they are completed (predominately documentaries, as well as horror flicks with well-known casts).

In the 1990s, it wasn't uncommon for an independent film to get several foreign distribution deals before going into production, and then U.S. distribution was always the icing on the cake later. Movies of all genres were able to benefit from this, as long as there were a few names attached to the script. Today, presales work a bit differently in that in order to get a foreign presale or confirmed foreign distribution in advance, you need to have a full cast of big names attached to your script in order for a distributor to prebuy for their territory.

However, there has been somewhat of a reverse model recently where filmmakers are able to get a U.S. DVD company to pre-buy distribution. Because physical DVD sales have been declining in recent years, the DVD industry is hungry for commercial products. They are therefore often willing to pre-buy distribution based on a commercial script with some B-list actors attached. In some cases, they will even pre-buy distribution for your project with no-name actors attached. In this situation, it helps if you have at least a track record of producing other films so that the U.S. DVD company can see that you have experience getting a movie in the can. Other than that, DVD companies have become much more willing in the past five years or so to engage in presales.

In securing distribution for your film during preproduction, one thing to beware of is that the amount of presale money is not going to finance a million-dollar budget. Most likely, you're looking at anywhere from $20K to possibly a few hundred thousand dollars, depending on your level of experience and the caliber of cast attached to your project. Note that it also helps if your production is a horror or action flick, because those are two genres that are proven to sell in the home-video marketplace.

If you are unable to secure distribution during preproduction, do not worry—you are not alone. Most filmmakers do not secure distribution for their movies at this stage; instead, they work on things that can significantly improve their chances of getting distribution after their film has been completed. Yes, there are some horror stories out there of filmmakers who sink their life savings into making their film, only to have it never see the light of distribution. However, I am a firm believer that there are precautions you can take in advance that will significantly increase your chances of making a movie that sells.

Get in Touch with the Market

In general, most filmmakers and producers are out of touch with market realities. And of course they are. It's not their job to know what particular market forces are in play at any given moment. However, if you spend just a little bit of time studying what kinds of films "sell," you will be able to glean enough insight to assist you in making educated decisions throughout your production process.

This may seem overly simplistic, but have a look at what's playing in the theaters, what's on the shelves in the video stores, and what's showing on cable. Check out the quality of these productions, the actors they're using, the artwork on the box. It's a cliche, but it's true: there has to be some kind of "hook" in order for your independent movie to find distribution. Whether it's star appeal, a popular genre such as horror, or a "niche" product (gay, sports, children, etc.), there has to be a special hook that makes your film stand out from the rest.

I was working with some filmmakers who wanted to make a romantic comedy to go straight to video and cable. Despite potential red flags, the filmmakers were very attached to their story and did some basic market research before even writing the script. They started by taking a trip to several video stores to see if there were any independent romantic comedies on the shelves that hadn't already had a U.S. theatrical release. There weren't. Next, the filmmakers made a target list of twenty cable networks where their movie might air, including HBO, Showtime, A&E, and IFC (Independent Film Channel), among others. They visited the web sites of these twenty cable networks and scrutinized their programming schedules.

What the filmmakers found was that most of these networks aired only movies that either had a major U.S. theatrical release or were one of their own original productions (which are becoming increasingly more common). In the rare cases where we saw an independent film on the program schedule that hadn't had a U.S. theatrical release, the picture had either a star-driven cast or was in the "family" genre category.

After researching video stores and cable networks, the filmmakers made a list of some romantic comedies they had seen in the past year. For each of these comedies, they indicated what the hook was that garnered distribution. The most common reason on the list was "cast," followed by "remake" or "adaptation" of some previous film or book.

The last thing they did in the market-research process was visit the American Film Market (AFM) (you can purchase a special producer's pass) and visit the booths of foreign sales agents and distribution companies to see what was being sold there. How many posters for romantic comedies did they find? Not many. In talking to a few foreign sales agents and even buyers visiting the market, the filmmakers ascertained that romantic comedies were not a popular sale at the time, and incidentally didn't translate well to overseas markets.

In this particular case, the results of a little basic market research were clear. The only circumstances under which it made sense to move forward with a romantic comedy would be if the filmmakers could raise enough money through private investors to attach at least two A-list cast members. Because the filmmakers were so committed to the project, they decided to give it a shot by increasing their budget substantially and hiring a distribution consultant to write a proper business plan. The plan was necessary so they could go to investors to raise the money needed to hire an A-list cast. The distribution consultant also helped by researching the amount of money that A-list cast members typically get paid for the minimum amount of shooting days, and so on.

With stars now attached to the project, the filmmakers were able to raise the necessary funds and secure U.S. DVD distribution.

Carefully Consider Genre and Format

Certain genres and formats do better than others at certain times. For example, horror films are doing well right now in the straight-to-video market, and there is demand for current-affairs documentaries by foreign broadcasters. Therefore, it makes sense to engage in market research for the particular genre you have in mind. If you find that there is low demand for your project, consider switching to a genre that is in higher demand. This, of course, will increase your chances of getting the movie distributed. And keep in mind that the cycle is continually changing—one week, horror is a hot commodity; the next week, comedy is in demand. The market is a fickle place—chances are, a project you put on hiatus can most likely be resurrected at a later date when there may be a place in the market for it.

However, there are some genres and formats that I find to be particularly in demand. Family films, animation, current-affairs documentaries, music documentaries, and action flicks (with B-stars or higher) are generally wildly popular genres nowadays—they always seem to find an audience. (Please keep in mind, those genres are just a partial list and represent what is currently happening. When it comes time to make your particular film, you should research the market and find out what the hot sellers are at that time.)

Something else to consider during preproduction is what your ultimate distribution goal is. For example, if your ultimate goal is to make a film for a theatrical release, you know that narrative features have a better shot than documentaries. Conversely, if you want a picture that gets international broadcast distribution, a documentary may be the way to go. So when considering the genre and format of the movie you want to make, also take into consideration your ultimate goal for distribution. If you want to make a film for the straight-to-video market, a film that has the potential to pay your investors back fast, then maybe a horror or action flick is the way to go.

Here is a short list of different distribution channels, along with the genres and formats that are likely to succeed in getting distribution through each channel.

- **U.S. theatrical distribution:** *feature films*—all genres; *documentaries*—music and political
- **U.S. broadcast distribution:** *feature films*—family; *documentaries*—music, sports, current events, historical, and natural history
- **U.S. DVD distribution:** *feature films*—action, horror, thriller, family, and animation; *documentaries*—music
- **Foreign distribution:** *feature films*—action, horror, thriller, and sci-fi; *documentaries*—music, current events, historical, and natural history

Casting for Distribution

One of the best investments you can make during preproduction of your project is casting. It can make or break distribution for your picture. Here's what to do: take the time and money to cast one or two A-list stars in your movie, even if it is for only one day of work. You will certainly get your money's worth. If you cannot get one or two A-list stars, then your next-best strategy is to get three to four B-list stars to act in your film.

For example, there was a filmmaker who had a dark-comedy script budgeted for $1 million. She had initial interest from some production companies who wanted to fund the project—on the condition that the filmmaker attach star names to the script.

She started by going through the budget and allotting $100K to hire two A-list stars for one day of work each. She made a cast wish list, and presented that list to a handful of domestic and international distributors for feedback. The distributors told the filmmaker which names had value in their markets. From that feedback, she narrowed down the list of which stars she could realistically go after. This "distributor-approved" cast list was passed on to the casting director, whose job it was to go and secure the talent. The good news is that the filmmaker knew going in that no matter which stars she ended up getting from the list, the picture was almost guaranteed distribution in certain territories.

The final result was that the filmmaker was able to get two A-list stars attached to the script. Each star committed to one day of work for $50K. This was enough to secure financing, and the film eventually got distribution in several territories, successfully recouped the initial investment of $1 million, and made a substantial profit.

Another option when it comes to casting, especially if you are dealing with a budget of less than $1 million, is to utilize B-list and current or past television actors and actresses. I have witnessed movies packed with these second-tier stars, and these pictures sell very well both domestically and overseas. Again, I recommend making a list of potential stars and getting feedback from domestic and foreign buyers, to learn which names will secure funding for your film.

For an example of how second-tier stars can be an ingredient to success, one need not look any further than John Travolta in *Pulp Fiction*, or John Ritter in *Sling Blade*. Prior to appearing in these movies, these two actors were considered to be has-beens. After the release of *Pulp Fiction* and *Sling Blade*, however, Travolta and Ritter found that their careers had been completely resurrected. If a distributor can "break" or revive a star's career as a result of your movie, you're basically set. If you've secured a U.S. domestic release and this happens, you can bet the international audience will come flocking.

When all else fails and you cannot even afford to hire B-list stars for a few days' work, at the very least take advantage of the Screen Actors Guild's low-budget schemes and cast professional talent in your film. Doing so will save you lots of time, money, and headaches. With SAG actors, you know from the beginning you are getting professional, experienced talent. And not too many producers and filmmakers know about SAG low-budget schemes or how to best utilize them. For more information, do yourself a favor and visit www.sagindie.org.

Paul Bales's film *Legion of the Dead*, was made for under $500 K utilizing one of the SAG low-budget schemes. Paul also happens to be the director of SAGIndie, so he was already very well versed in the advantages of using professional talent.

For his directorial debut, Bales made it a priority to use SAG actors. Under the SAG low-budget scheme, he was able to use professional actors at a fraction of the usual cost. For a total budget of less than $500 K, he had to cut corners somewhere, so Paul stuck to an eleven-day shooting schedule. Although this was definitely tight, he made up for it by using the SAG actors who were able to knock out their scenes faster, and consequently saved time in the end. He also shot on 35 mm film. Paul's movie got shelf space in Blockbuster, and the producers recouped their initial investment and are now making a profit.

One of the disadvantages, however, to using any SAG contract, be it low budget or otherwise, is that when your movie starts to make money, SAG will be the first in line to get paid, *not* the filmmaker. SAG will have written security agreements with the filmmaker to make sure of it. And if the filmmaker is lucky enough to have a big hit with their picture, SAG will require you to pay up. The devil, as always, is in the details.

An alternative to hiring SAG actors is the "financial core" model, which is based on a U.S. Supreme Court ruling that allows you to hire SAG actors and non-SAG actors for the same film. Many big-name stars work "financial core" all the time—all you have to do is ask.

Furthermore, from a distributor's standpoint, they hate having to sign SAG's distributor's assumption agreement. Collecting, paying out, and paying residuals on a low-budget indie is a waste of time for them. Unfortunately, the filmmaker will be left with paying for all this extra work.

The bottom line here is that using SAG contracts can work great for your film as long as the budget is big enough for this approach to make financial sense, with all the deferred payments you'll have to make later. So be sure to crunch the numbers before you sign any SAG contracts. And remember, even if you are going after A-list and B-list actors but not using SAG, always make sure the terms you negotiate with your actors are favorable (e.g., watch those deferred payments), so you can avert financial disaster later.

A question I get asked quite frequently is, Exactly how do I go about casting A-list or B-list stars for my indie film? Fortunately, there are several ways to go about it.

Hire a Casting Director

This may seem like an obvious solution, and it is—especially if you have the budget to hire someone with experience casting for independent films. What a good casting director can do for you is get your project to the top of actors' reading piles. Casting directors have relationships with agents and managers, so they can actually get to the actor much easier than you can on your own. In fact, most agents and managers won't even take your call unless you're a known casting director.

Casting directors also bring a lot of value to the table when it comes time to write offers and handle the paperwork (deferred payments, etc.) because they have experience in this too. They know how to run casting sessions and make listings in the breakdowns. Casting directors also may be aware of upcoming stars that you do not know about, and can make creative suggestions to fit your budget.

So in short, when it's time to go after your A- and B-list stars, a casting director can make this happen for you. But again, this option is open to you only if you have the budget to pay them. And the way to find an experienced casting director is to look at the credits of some recent successfully distributed indie films. You'll see some of the same names appear again and again. You can approach casting directors directly through their individual web sites.

Interview with Scout Masterson, C.S.A.
(Pirates of the Caribbean: At World's End, The Pursuit of Happiness, The Lake House)

How does hiring a professional casting director give an independent filmmaker an edge when trying to cast a film?
Since casting directors have a close relationship with many talent agents and managers, those relationships can be key to the film's success in attracting talent for the filmmaker, especially in the beginning stages of the project.

You've been involved in the casting of numerous big-studio movies and network TV shows, yet you cast independent films as well. What factors do you normally take into consideration when deciding to cast an indie?
First and foremost the script. If I don't feel a bond with the story and the writing . . . then I won't be passionate about the project—which is a must, since there's normally not a large amount at stake to be made while casting an independent film.

Once you come on board a project, what is the typical casting process like?
That's a tricky question, as it depends on what stage the project is in. Most low-budget independent movies don't have any talent attached, and in many cases need to have that talent to obtain any sort of financing. So in that case, the first step is to make lists of actors/actresses and have a creative, yet realistic, conversation with the director and producers to decide who the top choices are to target. After the choices are made—

normally several, since it's very rare that the top choice will attach them-selves unless it's a truly amazing and well-written script—then I contact the agents and managers of the actor to get them "excited" about the project, let them know I'm involved and how passionate I am about it, and then get the script off to them to read. That's basically the process until the lead(s) actors are attached.

While keeping the ultimate goal of distribution in mind, what do you think is a good casting strategy for an indie film?
I think the best way to answer this is to be creative and allow the financiers, producers, and director to communicate to me what their "needs" are to get the film distributed . . . meaning what talent means money for their financing, market to be distributed, etc.

How would you recommend a filmmaker work with a casting direc-tor on a shoestring budget?
There are several ways to do this. Some casting directors ask for a small fee up front, while others, if extremely passionate about the project, will work with the filmmaker to attach the leads before requiring any payments. In all cases, a "deal" is made for the casting director spelling out fees, billing, etc., and normally with independent movies, the casting director fee is set on a sliding scale depending on the budget. If the budget remains low, then the fee is set at that. But if, by chance, a big "star" is attached (i.e., Jim Carrey, Drew Barrymore, Cameron Diaz . . .), then there's a chance the budget will rise and the casting director fee does as well.

What is the biggest mistake you see filmmakers make when trying to cast an independent film?
I feel that many filmmakers are unrealistic about the talent that the project may/will attract. I also feel a big mistake is made when a really wonderful small film that should just be made and enjoyed is sometimes ruined when a big "star" is cast in the lead role. Obviously, most filmmakers would be ecstatic to have such a big name in their film, but sometimes it also ruins it for the audience and takes them out of the story. It's very important to be aware of the consequences of not choosing the right cast for the film, which is why it's important to have a passionate and creative casting direc-tor on board.

What's the best way for an indie filmmaker to go about finding a casting director and getting in touch with them?
There are several ways to go about finding the best casting director for the film. A filmmaker can submit the project to the Casting Society of America

(C.S.A.), and they send out an email to all members of any new projects submitted this way. All of the information is on the web site (www. castingsociety.com). Another avenue a filmmaker can take is to watch the films that they enjoy the casting of and try to contact the casting director of that film. Or, of course, if the filmmaker has any connections with talent agents or managers, that's also a great resource.

Submit Offers to Agents

If you don't have the budget to hire a casting director, but have some potential financing lined up, you can always make your own cast wish list and submit offers to agents and managers yourself. Be warned, though—you really need to know what you're doing here, because you will be disregarded as an amateur if you don't get it right.

First of all, in order to find out who represents the actor to whom you wish to make an offer, you can call around to the major agencies (Creative Artists, International Creative Management, William Morris, United Talent, and Endeavor) and simply ask the receptionist, "Do you represent so-and-so?" They will tell you yes or no. If the answer is yes, ask who the responsible agent is. If the answer is no, say thank you and move on.

Also note that each of the big agencies has an independent-film division. These divisions will have one or two agents whose job it is to speak with independent producers and pass material on to the actors' responsible agents. So another tactic you can try when calling an agency directly is to ask for the independent-film department, and then go from there.

You an also utilize web sites such as www.whorepresents.com or www.imdbpro.com. For $10 to $12 per month, you can have access to an entire database of actors and who their representatives are, along with contact details and other information. Still another option for finding out your chosen actors' representation is to call SAG Actors to Locate service, and they will give you the representation they have on file for up to three actors you request at a time.

Once you find out who the agent is for the actor to whom you wish to submit an offer, then you call that agent and ask if so-and-so is available for whenever you plan on shooting. They will tell you yes or no and/or tell you the actor's availability. You can tell the agent you will be submitting an offer for your film.

From there, you will need help from either a lawyer, casting director, or distribution consultant on how to draft a written offer. You don't want to seem like an amateur here, so make sure you get this part right. Once you get your formal offer on paper worked out, you send it in to the agent with a copy of your screenplay and other details of the film. With a written offer in hand, they are obliged to present it to the client. Remember that you should always add some kind of "condition" that would allow you to duck out of the offer if necessary. It's like buying a house with a contingency (e.g., if you fix up the bathrooms, then I'll buy it). This condition is usually disguised as "based on the positive outcome of a meeting with the actor."

And beware that the agent may ask for a "pay-or-play" offer for their client. What this means is that you pay the actor's fee whether or not you end up casting them in your film. So be careful of the pay-or-play offers!

After you submit an offer to an agent for their client, you wait . . . and probably wait some more . . . until you hear back yes or no. It may take two days; it may take two months. You can be a squeaky wheel if you want, but you must also be patient.

It is not O.K. to present multiple offers at the same time for the same role. So unfortunately, you will have to wait until you hear back from your first choice before approaching your second choice. However, you can work on casting multiple roles at the same time, so hopefully you have three or four offers out there for the three or four roles you are casting with A-list or B-list actors. And if you do decide to present multiple offers at once, by all means keep your mouth shut about it. If the agents with whom you are dealing find this out, they won't be happy and can automatically decline your offer to their client.

Interview with Julie Colbert, William Morris Agency

If an independent filmmaker wants to make an offer to one of your clients, what is the standard protocol they should abide by?
Tell the truth. Don't try to snow me. If you don't have the money yet, say so. It can be hard to gauge the viability of an independent project for an agent at all stages, and very often we become partners with the independent producer when a client wants to do a film. So, if I realize you've fudged the truth on something, I will be less likely to trust you, and therefore less likely to want to be in business with you. Especially if something goes wrong, as it often does. I look for good scripts. You'd be shocked at how few and far between they are, and when something is interesting, I'm happy to put the work in to try and get the money and other cast with you. Also, if you have a project for a client who really wants to work, I'll work hard on it with you as well.

In general, should an independent filmmaker "start at the top" by making offers to your A-list clients? Or what about B-level stars or TV or music stars who might want to work in film?
Be realistic. If you have a stunning script with some kind of pedigree, then it's definitely worth taking a shot with an A-lister. Otherwise, it's often a complete waste of time for both of us. Busy A-list clients don't have as much time to read. I usually will read everything that comes in that's at all real. I will then forward it on to my client and/or their manager with my opinion. If my opinion is that the project is mediocre, it goes way down on the pile of things to do, and it tends to sit there and sit there. On the other hand, if I'm really working hard to find something for a client who maybe doesn't have as much brewing, and you bring me a viable idea, I read it right away, encourage the client to do the same. and, if we like it, we're off to the races. Alternatively, if my client doesn't like it, I will bring it to my colleagues for their clients and make sure to note that you are open to ideas . . . not just A-listers. Also, if you have a great project, it will get recognized once it gets read. In our staff meetings, if someone announces that they've read an excellent script, everybody listens (if you have any credibility at all) and takes a look themselves and tries to get the project going.

What is an acceptable offer amount for a day or two's work on an indie film?
There is a huge variance here. Again, if the script or the director are interesting, a client will sometimes take less money because it's a "passion

project." If the client is so-so on the script and you are using their name to sell it, expect to pay for that privilege. Also, condense your dates for a name as much as possible. It's much easier for someone to do something if it's three consecutive days rather than three days throughout the shoot. I've had name clients get paid low-budget SAG scale for a project they loved and easily fit in their schedule, and I've had clients get paid $500 K for a week plus a back end because the producer was using the name to sell the project foreign.

Are there any other bits of advice you can offer filmmakers who want to work with professional/agency-represented talent? Anything they should avoid?
It's good to be aggressive, but don't call every day looking for updates. These things take time, and sometimes when people get pushed too much, they pass on the project just because they don't want to deal with it anymore.

Exploit Your Contacts and Go for Out-of-Work Actors

If you don't have the budget to hire a casting director, and you aren't anywhere near having potential financing lined up, and in fact you need one or two name actors attached to your project in order to attract financing at all, then you should start exploiting every contact you have as well as targeting out-of-work actors. When contacting out-of-work actors, just be careful they don't know you're contacting them for that reason. In other words, make them believe they are your first choice. You'll get them for next to nothing, and they'll be very happy to work for you.

In terms of exploiting your contacts for your A-list cast choices, take your cast wish list, arm yourself with who the representatives are for your top choices, and because you are not in a position to make a written offer, find out if anyone you know is personally acquainted with any of the agents or managers involved. Then see if you can get personally referred to them. If you manage to get a personal referral to an agent or manager, be honest with them about the fact that you do not have financing in place, but you would like to submit your script to their client for consideration.

When contacting agents or managers without financing in place, you should definitely be targeting underemployed actors whom you haven't seen in a while (think Burt Reynolds in *Boogie Nights*). Actors who are not working or getting any offers have very anxious agents, so the agents will be motivated to present your script to them even though you cannot provide a written offer. It's called getting in through the back door.

One other question I seem to get asked all the time is, How do I know which second-tier or B-list actors are currently "selling"? The best way to determine which second-tier and B-list actors you should be targeting for your movie is to take a trip to the video store and see who appears over and over again on straight-to-video new releases. You'll be able to tell very quickly which B-list actors are selling videos (by virtue of the fact that they have shelf space), and therefore you'll know that by casting them, at least you can be almost guaranteed a U.S. video release. Go after these B-list actors— they are very valuable!

Another way to determine which B-list actors to target so that you can attract financing and distribution is to do more extensive research and analyze which of these second-tier stars are appearing on straight-to-cable movies, foreign video releases, and so on.

Interview with Paul Bales, independent filmmaker and director of SAGIndie

Paul, tell us a little bit about your movie *Legion of the Dead*. I understand you had a budget of less than $200K, and you were still able to shoot on 35 mm film! What were some of your secrets for getting this thing in the can on time and on budget?

Enormous amounts of caffeine! The budget was less than $200K, and we did shoot it on 3 mm. I guess the biggest secret, which was also the biggest challenge, was the schedule. We shot the film in eleven days (we were originally scheduled for twelve, but lost one due to rain). We were shooting between ten and fourteen pages a day, with one or two takes per setup, and *a second unit shooting continuously. Preparation was key. I had done storyboards and shot lists for every scene . . . and although we rarely had time to shoot as I had planned, I learned that all of that prep work was necessary on the set in being able to know what shots were critical, which ones you had to get. It also helped that my DP, Megan Schoenbachler, and my first AD, Justin Jones, had a lot of experience and are both geniuses! We worked together really well and spent each morning planning the day.*

What was your greatest challenge in making a picture with such a low budget?

Again, time. As a first-time director, I certainly made a lot of mistakes and learned a lot of lessons, but I feel pretty strongly that almost everything in the final film that I am unhappy with could have been resolved had we just had more time.

I hear you were able to use SAG actors in your movie. What were some of the advantages to working with SAG actors? How does SAG work with low-budget filmmakers to make working with SAG actors a reality?

I had to use SAG actors. My "day job" is running SAGIndie, the educational/outreach program for independent producers. It's my job to convince low-budget filmmakers to use SAG actors, so if I had done a nonunion film, I would have been crucified on the roof of the SAG building. The advantages to using SAG actors are enormous. SAG actors understand the vocabulary of filmmaking, they know how to find their marks, they come to the set on time and prepared (having memorized their lines and studied their characters). SAG actors make the director's job very easy, because they have experience. Yet, even though Bruce Boxleitner, who was in my film, has acted in more movies than I've seen, he still listened to me and took my direction. SAG makes it easy for filmmakers to use SAG actors by offering five different low-budget agreements for films at every budget level; from "no-budget" short films, to $2.5 million–dollar features.

Tell us about the planned distribution for your film, and how you got distribution.

My situation was a little unique, because the company that produced the film, The Asylum (www.theasylum.cc_), is also a distributor. They have output deals with the major video stores and international markets, so distribution for my film was pretty much a foregone conclusion (although the stores could have refused to take the film if they didn't like it). As a film-

maker, I would definitely recommend working with a company that has distribution deals in place. Beyond that, I would also recommend making a film that is marketable. Don't get me wrong . . . I love smart independent films . . . dramas, etc., but unless they do really well in the right festivals, they are really hard to sell. If a filmmaker is really serious about making a commercially successful independent film, they should make a commercial film. My film is a genre film: horror . . . and I'm told that it's really hard not to sell a low-budget horror film. . . .

Financing Strategies for Distribution

When trying to finance your independent film, It pays to raise the extra money in order to hire a professional cast, shoot on film or HD instead of video, and in general make a better movie. I know many filmmakers who follow the "down and dirty" philosophy and pull together whatever funds they have, slap something together on a miniDV camera using their relatives as actors, and then expect their movie to get distribution. As a general rule, this doesn't work.

I was working with a filmmaker once who wanted to make a movie for half a million dollars. Looking at his budget, I saw that almost nothing was allotted toward cast, and that they planned to shoot the film on miniDV. With this type of movie—a drama, shot on DV with no recognizable cast—it would be nearly impossible to recoup the $500K investment through sales. I encouraged them to double the movie's budget. This may seem counterintuitive, but here's the reasoning: stepping up to a $1 million budget would allow the filmmaker to substantially increase production quality, shoot on 35 mm film (but not produce a negative), and hire two or three A-list cast members for leading roles and pay them for a few days' work. A film with high production quality and an A-list cast has an infinitely greater chance of recouping several times the initial investment.

In the end, the filmmakers first attached two A-list stars to the project (this took a few months, but was well worth the time), then raised their budget accordingly (to $1.5 million) to pay for the actors, budgeted to shoot in high definition, and eventually secured distribution.

In terms of financing, these particular filmmakers used private investors to fund their $1.5 million budget. But how do you jump from a $500K budget to a $1.5 million budget if you don't have any private investors on board? And if you can't manage to finance a $1 million budget or higher, how do you make the best of a $500K or less budget and still get distribution?

Because there are entire books dedicated to the subject of financing independent films, I'll keep my suggestions focused on what I call distribution-related financing. Distribution-related financing options include the following:

Presales

As stated earlier, a presale is literally a sale of your film to a particular territory before the film is made. For example, if you have a script with some actors attached to the key roles, you are eligible for a presale. A U.K. distributor might assess your film package and think that it has potential salability, and offer to prebuy distribution rights for their territory.

When a distributor prebuys rights, it is advantageous to them because if they know in advance that you have a hot property, they can secure the distribution rights up front instead of waiting until it's completed and then having to compete with all the other distributors in their territory for the distribution rights. For this reason, distributors also tend to get a good deal when they prebuy their territory, because they are taking a risk that once executed, the film will be the hot property they thought it was and be able to recoup their advance through ticket sales.

Presales have become more difficult in the past ten years because distributors, particularly foreign distributors, have gotten badly burned by prebuying into pictures that have turned out to be total flops. In many instances, distributors have lost their entire investment. As a result and over the years, foreign distributors have tacked on more and more technical requirements for a presale. In other words, instead of just having an A-list cast attached, as was once the case, you now have to have an experienced director and producer attached with proven track records. These extra requirements further ensure that the project not only has the stars to attract an audience, but will be executed well and the film will actually be seen to completion, make it into the theaters, and garner ticket sales.

For obvious reasons, presales are advantageous to filmmakers. For one thing, it's a way to raise money for your movie while securing distributors at the same time. Another advantage is that a presale gives your film cachet in that if someone believed in your picture enough to prebuy for their territory, it is very likely that other distributors from other territories will be attracted to a presale as well. Pretty soon, by preselling off a few territories, you can raise all the money for your film with the assurance that it will be seen in those countries.

Presales are generally made with the help of foreign sales agents because they are the ones that have the relationships with foreign distributors. However, you may be able to secure your own presale by submitting to the distributors directly. Be warned, though, that this form of financing has become extremely rare these days, and isn't even worth considering unless you have an A-list cast and are a producer or director with a proven track record.

The one exception that I've seen happening over the past few years is if you have a film packaged with proven B-list straight-to-video stars, U.S. DVD distributors have been stepping up to the plate to prebuy their rights. So if you're not in a position to get any kind of A-list stars attached to your project and you want to explore presale financing, then your best bet is to find three or four of those straight-to-video stars and attach them to your movie.

International Coproductions

An international coproduction is a form of a presale where the distributor takes a much larger stake in the film, and in fact becomes a coproducer on the movie. International coproductions grew out of presales. When distributors started getting badly burned, they decided that if they took a greater involvement in the project, it could act as insurance that the film was executed properly. With this further insurance, at least distributors could somewhat rely on making their investment back.

International coproductions, like presales, are very rare these days, and pretty much carry the same requirements as a presale in terms of a salable project and A-list cast potential. However, with the increase in demand for nonfiction programming by cable and satellite networks, I have actually seen an increase in international coproductions for documentaries and special-interest films that fit a programming mandate. For example, when a new travel network began broadcasting in Germany, they were so hungry for travel documentaries that they entered into several international coproduction deals to fill their programming pipeline and ensure that they would have enough shows in the coming year to air to their burgeoning audience.

Sometimes you can finance a film with one international coproduction, or several at a time, and as with a presale, a distributor also retains the distribution rights for their territory in a coproduction arrangement.

Also, if you're seeking an international coproduction as a way to finance your movie, your best bet is to work with a foreign sales agent, because they have the relationships and know the intricacies involved in a coproduction deal, including all the contractual issues.

Interview with Ashley Luke, acquisitions for Fortissimo Films (*For Your Consideration, Shortbus, 2046*)

Tell us about Fortissimo Films. I know you are one of the most prestigious foreign sales agencies, but are you a production company as well? Where are you based?

Fortissimo Films was founded in 1991. We are well known for our passion for film and for nurturing up-and-coming directors and producers. We have excellent relationships with key international distributors, film festivals, and local and international journalists—which helps us in the promotion, marketing, and selling of the films we represent. We have been involved in production as producers and as executive producers. Personally, I am based in Sydney, but the head office is in Amsterdam, with the other key offices being in Hong Kong, London, and New York. We also have agents in Tokyo and Beijing.

2. Speaking of acquisitions, how and where do you acquire most of your films?
We are sent a lot of scripts, and a lot of projects are now acquired at script stage. There are also screenings throughout the year when filmmakers send us their finished films to screen. We attend all of the major festivals and markets, where we also screen films that are still available for sales representation and have meetings with producers and discuss their new projects.

Do you acquire only finished films, or scripts as well? If so, what are the requirements for each?
If we acquire a finished film, we prefer that it has not been shown in any festivals. This then gives us the opportunity to premiere the film in the appropriate way and at the appropriate festival. We like to work with films as early as possible. On projects from a script stage, we like to have a complete package. That is, budget, any financing in place, director must be attached, and if possible (but not always a must), some idea of cast—in fact, any information, like a director's statement, copies of their previous work we can screen, when the film is intended to be made, etc.

What do you look for in an indie film? Must there be A-list stars attached? Or must it have won at a major festival? Or does an indie with no names, but one that's just a great film, have a shot with you?
We are always on the lookout for something different (isn't everyone?). Something with a strong story. A story with heart and one that will speak to a wide audience. We represent a lot of films without the so-called A-list cast, and if they are strong and different enough, they can succeed. Obviously, having a named cast can help a film enormously, but it is not always a condition with us. We certainly do represent independent films with no names, and will continue to do so.

How has the foreign sales landscape changed over the years in terms of the types of films you acquire?
It has changed somewhat. The independent scene is a much tougher marketplace now, and it doesn't seem to be getting any easier. I think the change

with us has also been, in part, a natural progression of the company. We have always been known for dealing with foreign-language films, in particular Asian films, and we continue with that. In the last few years, we have taken on many more English-language films and have achieved great success. For most independent distributors, it has become nearly impossible to sell art-house films to free and pay television, and therefore their acquisition policies have become much more conservative.

Any suggestions for filmmakers who want to approach you with their film? What is the preferred method and protocol? Anything they should avoid?
Most of my correspondence throughout the year is by email, as it is with my colleagues. If a filmmaker wants us to consider their finished film or script, then an initial email to us with information about the film or the project is good. I always stress that if you can find a name of someone in the company to address it to, this means a lot. We get a lot of anonymous emails, and they are not always dealt with first! Be concise, but at the same time give a good idea of what you have. We do not accept unsolicited material, so please don't send your film in without prior notice or email your script. Check out the Fortissimo web site; it paints a very good picture of the kind of films we work with. If you do not do your homework and send us a film or project that is absolutely not our sort of thing, you are not only wasting your time but ours as well. These rules also apply for personal meetings at festivals and markets.

Any tips for filmmakers who want to make a picture that has potential for foreign distribution? Is it all horror and action films everyone is after?
No it isn't, thankfully. Like us, our distributors are always on the lookout for different and standout films. There are some tried and tested types of films, and there are trends, but these change in time, and we have to change with the times. There are still a lot of low-budget films being made, and a lot of them are awfully good. Have decent production values, make sure you have a budget for all the items that will be required of you by a sales agent, and in turn a distributor, and if possible talk to a sales agent as early in the game as possible. It is invaluable to have an agent on board and working with you through the life of the film.

Of course, aside from these two forms of distribution-related financing, there are the tried-and-true financing methods—including seeking out private investors, raising money from friends and family, and maxing out your credit cards. However, with those forms of film financing, you do not have any guaranteed distribution as you do with presales and coproductions, so remember that it's money you'll have to repay later, after you make sales of your picture.

If you get to a point in the process of raising money where it doesn't look like you're going to raise enough to hire A-list cast and really go for a high-level production, you can take a Plan B approach and stick with a budget of less than $250K. In my opinion, that is a good number to adhere to, because if the film turns out well, you can at least be sure to recoup that amount in a U.S. DVD distribution deal over time. So at the very least, you can create a business plan based on a $250K budget and give realistic sales projections that will show any investor that he or she can make that amount back.

Creating a Trailer or Promo to Raise Presale and International Coproduction Money

In terms of raising presale and international coproduction money, one effective way to accomplish this is by cutting together a short trailer or promo of your movie to show to potential distributors. You might be thinking, How are you supposed to cut together a trailer or promo if you haven't shot the picture yet?

If you are making a documentary film, for example, one way to accomplish this is through the use of stock footage. For instance, if you are trying to raise money for a documentary on the Gulf War, you could go to broadcast archives such as CNN or the BBC, both which have footage-licensing arms, and order screening cassettes of programs relating to the Gulf War. From these collections of tapes, you can easily cut together a professional-looking promo piece to illustrate to distributors the movie you are going to make. You can even make the selling point that you will in fact be using this very prestigious footage in your film. Employing stock footage from places such as the BBC, CNN, and other archives adds credibility and a professional look to your project. And it's a great tool for raising presale and coproduction moneys.

If you are making a narrative feature instead of a documentary, obviously the situation is a little different. Licensing historical stock footage doesn't really pertain to making a trailer or promo for a narrative feature film. However, I have seen many filmmakers get their actors together for a day of shooting, and shoot a few sample scenes from the picture, enough to edit together a professional-looking sample of what you are going to accomplish with the full-length feature. You may have already made a short film of the feature you want to make. Short films can be great tools in this capacity as well. As you can imagine, visual samples go a long way in communicating your capabilities to potential distributors and coproducers.

Set Money Aside for the Last Mile

One other thing to keep in mind when financing your project for future distribution is to set aside adequate money for all your deliverables. I cover deliverables in more detail in Part Five, but let me just touch on what's important to think about while you're raising money in preproduction.

- **Music and Effects (M&E tracks):** M&E tracks can cost anywhere from $5K to $10K and up, depending on the sound mixer you are using and the quality of production sound he or she has to work with.
- **Film Print:** If you plan on outputting your movie to film, transfer costs to a print (if you didn't shoot on 35 mm to begin with)—plus the cost of the print and all the lab fees—can cost anywhere from a few thousand dollars up to, say, $30K to $50K, depending on the lab you're using, the length of your picture, and many other factors.
- **Advertising:** If you decide to self-distribute your project and need to purchase advertising to promote it, this can run you anywhere from a few thousand dollars to a few hundred thousand dollars, depending what markets you are advertising in (obviously, Los Angeles or New York are much more expensive markets to advertise in than Chapel Hill or Portland are),

and if you are utilizing print, Internet, or grassroots advertising campaigns.

- **Publicity:** If you plan to hire a publicist to help you with advertising, promotions, and publicity, plan on setting aside anywhere from a few thousand dollars to $10K and up, depending on how long you plan to keep the publicist on retainer, what you are requiring them to do, if they are freelance or belong to a big PR firm, and so forth.
- **Music Clearances:** If you plan on your movie's using any music that is from an artist with a record deal or publishing deal, plan on setting aside anywhere from a few thousand dollars to a few hundred thousand dollars. The amount will depend on how popular the artists are, whether the songs you wish to license are big hits, how much the record labels and publishers decide to charge you, and how well you can negotiate with them to keep licensing fees to a minimum.
- **Stock Footage:** Even if you don't think you'll need to license stock footage for your film, I would set aside anywhere from $2K to $10K in case you need to fill in any "holes" in your movie that you didn't anticipate. Stock footage is a great tool during postproduction for enhancing your picture and filling in gaps, but it costs money. So be prepared by having a little in the budget expressly for licensing stock footage.
- **Film Festivals:** Don't forget to set aside a few hundred or a few thousand for film festival submission fees, depending on how many festivals you plan to submit to, and which ones.

I've seen many instances when a filmmaker doesn't think about raising extra money for these items during preproduction, and then suffers for it later. For instance, one of the most common and worst examples I've seen is that a filmmaker actually gets interest in his or her movie from a foreign distributor—but then has no money to go back and make the M&E tracks that they never made in the first place, because they didn't plan ahead and set aside money to make them during postproduction. When there are no M&E tracks, the foreign buyer refuses the sale, because the M&E tracks are how they make their foreign-language dub. Whereas a lot of pictures imported to the United States are shown with subtitles, this is not true for the rest of the world. In most countries, any film in a foreign language is dubbed. This is pretty much the case in most territories. Without the M&E track, the sale will be lost because a buyer will have a film they cannot dub, and therefore the movie is essentially useless to them. M&E tracks are expensive yet necessary, and foreign buyers are not in the habit of putting up money for these tracks to be added on. When they buy a picture, they generally buy it "as is," save for the actual foreign-language dub.

I've also seen disasters centered around music clearances. If you get a distributor interested in your movie as a result of having used a screener with uncleared music, they will not take kindly to your removing those songs. They will assume that you paid the clearance costs, and if you cannot offer to pay them at this stage, sadly, the sale of your film won't go through.

How Much Will I Make? Realistic Sales Projections for Your Film

I fully recommend figuring out sales projections of your movie before you go into production. Not only will this allow you to raise the proper amount of financing for your project, but you will have a better chance of paying back your investors later. It can sometimes be a rude awakening once the distribution deals start closing. What you thought you might make in terms of sales revenues at the outset of production might not be the case at all. In fact, most filmmakers are grossly unaware of what realistic sales projections are in the first place.

Any sales projections charts that I have seen published in books and magazines I find to be unrealistic for independent films. The table I have created on page 36 gives the low range and high range of what realistic acquisition prices are, based on my experience selling pictures to DVD and broadcast buyers worldwide.

Keep in mind that the low range of numbers represents a film with *no* stars attached whatsoever. The high range of numbers represent a film with two or three B-level names attached.

If you are lucky enough to have A-list stars in your film, then the sky's the limit! In that case, you're looking at possibly a $1 million or more buyout—could even be several million. If you have an A-list cast, you have a great chance of getting an all-rights deal, and won't need to worry about sales figures for individual territories such as the ones below.

If you have no stars attached to your film, or only B-level stars attached, why do you need to worry about these sales figures? For two reasons. The first reason is because, as I said before, hopefully you will take these into consideration *before* making your movie. If you do, you will already have raised the appropriate amount of money for your project—an amount that realistically can be paid back to an investor through distribution deals. The second reason is because if you've already made your film, and didn't project sales from the beginning, then at least you know roughly what you're in for, and won't blame your sales agent for telling you they got only $5K for your movie in Thailand!

Over the years, I've heard so many filmmakers complain about the prices that their sales agents and reps accept when they close distribution deals. The fact is, most of the time the sales agent or rep is just getting what the market will bear in terms of price. Remember, it's in their best interest, too, to get the highest possible price for your movie. After all, the sales agent or rep works on a commission basis. The only time they accept a price below normal market rates is when they do a package deal. This means selling several films in their catalog in a package to one buyer. The buyer benefits from a volume discount—but you do not.

Once again, the table below is just a general guideline that contains very conservative estimates. If your film wins big awards at one of the Tier 1 film festivals, then these amounts could double or even triple. Likewise, if any of the stars in your movie suddenly become really famous, that, too, could increase these projections considerably.

Also note that the term "ask prices" represents what you will be asking for when soliciting an offer from a distributor. This is the high end of the revenue you can expect. In contrast, the term "take prices" means the lowest amount you'd be willing to take from a distributor. This is the low end of the revenue you can expect. Simply put, these are the best-case and worst-case revenue scenarios for each territory listed.

Territory	Ask Prices ($K)	Take Prices ($K)	Sold	Pending Company	NOTES
Africa	3	1			
Australia	10	5			
Austria	(with Germany)				
Baltics	10	2.5			
Belgium	(with France & Netherlands)				
Brazil	10	2.5			
Canada	(with U.S.)				
Canada, French	(with France)				
China	10	2.5			
Commonwealth of Independent States	(with Russia)				
Denmark	20	5			
Eastern Europe	15	5			
Finland	15	5			
France	20	5			
Germany	25	5			
Hong Kong	10	2.5			
Hungary	10	2.5			
India	10	2.5			
Indonesia	5	2			
Israel	10	2.5			
Italy	20	5			
Japan	25	5			
Korea	15	3			
Latin America	10	5			
Malaysia	5	1.5			
Middle East	10	5			
Netherlands	10	2.5			
New Zealand	5	2			
Norway	15	5			
Philippines	5	1.5			
Poland	10	2.5			
Portugal	10	2.5			
Russia	10	5			
Singapore	5	1			
South Africa	5	1.5			
Spain	10	2			
Sweden	15	5			
Switzerland	(with Germany & France)				
Taiwan	5	1.5			
Thailand	5	2.5			
Turkey	10	2.5			
United Kingdom	50	5			
United States	100	10			
Totals	538	127			

Make a Business Plan for Your Film

If you want to raise the appropriate amount of money for your movie—which is to say, an amount that is in line with future sales revenue—I recommend creating a professional business plan for your project. Short, sweet, and to the point is the general format you should use. Potential investors want to know three things: (1) What is your project? (2) How much do you need? and (3) How am I going to get paid back?

I have significant experience partnering with filmmakers to create business plans in order to raise financing for their projects. Although it can be a very lengthy process, and I recommend you work with a professional on this, here is the general outline I suggest using when creating your plan:

I. **Executive Summary:** A summary of your production company
II. **Management/Organization:** A summary of who the people are in your orgainization—your bio and the bios of any other key personnel or crew
III. **The Project:** A brief (keep it to one page) synopsis of your project
IV. **Production Strategy:** Your cast wish list with previous credits, along with your proposed production and postproduction schedules
V. **Distribution Strategy:** Your proposed strategy for distributing the film, including festival submissions
VI. **Request For Funding:** How much you are asking for
VII. **Recoupment Strategy:** How and when you plan to repay the investors
VIII. **Worldwide Sales Projections:** A chart stating realistic worldwide sales estimates for your film so that your potential investors can see where the money will be coming from

Suggested Exercises for Part Two

1. Go to the video store and browse several straight-to-video titles. Alternatively, you can browse web sites (such as Amazon) that

sell DVDs. The way to determine if a title is straight-to-video is to notice whether or not you ever saw it out in the theaters, and then you can confirm this by going to the film's web site. If there has been (or will be) a theatrical release, they will usually have the information there. Are there any recurring patters in genre and format? How about stars that appear again and again? Write a paragraph explaining your findings by listing the titles of these straight-to-video titles, genre, starts, and distribution company. The purpose of this exercise is to market-research in advance what kind of titles are getting distribution, what stars are obviously selling, and which companies are putting them out in the market. In completing this exercise, maybe there are some actors you will discover that can at least guarantee a straight-to-video deal as insurance to your investors.

Repeat this exercise for the following two other market segments:

1. Straight-to-cable market (for example, see which films went straight-to-cable on Sundance Channel, Lifetime, HBO, IFC, etc.)
2. Platform theatrical release

2. To learn more about how presales work, contact three foreign or domestic acquisition executives by email, and ask them if they would ever consider a presale and under what conditions. Start making a database of companies that are willing to do presales. This information is golden!

— 3 —

Production Geared Toward Distribution

Part Two touched on things you could do during preproduction that would increase the chances of your movie's getting distribution: market research, raising enough money to make a quality film, distribution-related financing, and putting money aside for the last mile.

In Part Three, I will cover what you can do during the production process to increase the chances of acquiring distribution for your picture. Taking the time to make a few smart choices during production as well will save you headaches down the line when you finally finish the project and start looking into distribution options.

This is not to say that your film cannot get distribution deals while you are actually in production, because I've seen that happen on a few occasions. I was working with a filmmaker once who was in production of a sci-fi thriller. He had tried to secure U.S. and foreign presales during preproduction, but didn't have any luck because he was a first-time director with no high-profile cast attached to his film. He ended up raising the money for his project through a private investor and then began production.

About three-quarters of the way through production, the filmmaker's editor cut together a promo piece from all the footage they had captured. By this time, they already had the best action sequences in the can anyway.

After the promo piece was completed, the producer began shopping it around to distributors. He caught the eye of a U.S. DVD distributor who closed on a distribution deal and advanced him some money (which sure came in handy during postproduction). The producer was up front with the distributor and told him that they were still shooting, but gave him a realistic time frame for delivery of the film. The DVD distributor and producer agreed on an acceptable delivery date, and everyone was happy.

This is just one example of how you can not only start gearing up for distribution during production, but actually go out and shop distribution deals as well. If you are not in a position to cut together a professional-looking trailer or promo from the material you have shot, then there are other things you can do during production to at least give you a head start on distribution for when your film is completed.

The following are some things you can do to help ensure distribution during the production stage:

Shooting Format

One of the best investments you can make in your movie is shooting on film or high definition (HD) rather than on video. Many filmmakers are tempted to save money on production by shooting their movie on digital video (DV). However, by shooting on film (16 mm or 35 mm) or HD, your picture will have an infinitely better shot at getting distribution. Here's why: when DV became popular, the barriers to making a movie came way down. Aspiring filmmakers were finally free to go and make their movie for significantly less money. This was both a blessing and a curse. The blessing is obvious: The curse is that the market became flooded with independent films—so much so that after a few years, demand dropped, and so did the prices that buyers were willing to pay. Furthermore, the quality of independent films on the market plummeted. Currently, one of the first questions distributors ask me when I'm presenting a film is, "What was this shot on?" In almost every case, they immediately reject a movie shot on video unless there are several A-list cast attached. This rule isn't absolute, but at present, nine times out of ten, buyers and distributors will reject a film shot on DV. The exception is niche projects–such as children's movies or family films—where product is in high demand.

It should also be noted that HD is a new alternative to shooting on film, and is becoming widely accepted by domestic and international distributors. But beware—by the time you convert your HD movie to film and strike a print, you may well end up spending the same amount of money as if you had shot on film in the first place.

Regardless of those facts, the upsides to shooting on HD are the following:

- No film costs or processing costs during production, or during most of postproduction
- Instant replay of the takes
- Extra takes with no additional film costs or processing costs
- Relatively inexpensive color correction and special effects
- Vast control over color manipulation and special effects
- Cheap, easy, fast ability to reedit (while, say, on the festival circuit) in response to audience feedback (i.e., tweaking is cheap and easy—no need to recut negative to make a new interpositive and new print)

The bottom line is that if shot correctly and with the right equipment, DP and video tech, HD can look as good as film.

Something else to keep in mind if shooting on high definition is that there are several different formats of HD, and new ones popping up all the time. If possible, always go with the highest-quality camera and shooting resolution that your budget allows, because by the time you release your film, there is likely to be a newer and higher-quality HD format on the market.

The Importance of Stills

Another great investment during production is taking still photographs of your actors "in action" on the movie set. If you can afford it, hire a professional photographer for this task, especially someone who's had experience shooting film stills. His or her stills will have a more professional look to them, and you'll find that this is important later. If you cannot hire a pro, study some film stills yourself—you can find many online with a simple search, or visit a movie memorabilia shop where you'll find bins and bins of stills. By looking at a few, you'll quickly learn just what a proper still looks like.

A good set of still photographs is important for two reasons. One, you can use them later when developing the campaign for your picture as well as for your web site. Two, sales agents and distributors will demand high-resolution still photos as part of your "deliverables"—items you must deliver to them upon signature of the distribution contract and prior to their making sales. Sales agents and distributors need a good set of still photographs in order to develop their own marketing campaigns, sales sheets, and posters. Failing to provide these makes the sales agents' job that much harder when they try to sell your movie. Distributors need all materials presented to them in as clear and concise a package as possible (and they do expect a package). If you don't provide a complete package, your film will be a less attractive candidate for distribution before they even know anything about it. Distributors always have a lot of choices in front of them. Doing the little things that make marketing as easy as possible for distributors will automatically increase your chances of getting them interested in your film. Ideally, you should shoot your stills with a high-end digital camera and deliver them on a DVD to the distributor.

Starting Publicity During Production: Get the Buzz Going

During production is actually a great time to start creating a buzz for your film. This can later be used as a marketing tool for sales agents and distributors. Creating a buzz during production also helps build your audience far in advance so that by the time you are finished with your picture, you already have a following and people who want to see it. This can be valuable in terms of marketing to distributors or sales reps, because if you can show them you already have an audience for your movie, obviously your project will be more appealing to them.

With today's technology, there are several ways you can start getting a buzz for your film. They include the following:

- Create a web site or blog.
  A web site or blog can be an invaluable tool during production in terms of building an audience. And because there are so many free services out there, it makes it even better (try Google and Yahoo!, which each have free blog software and web building tools).

  Start by doing production diaries—daily, every other day, or just a couple times a week. Add snippets of video or stills, and when you have enough footage, a little trailer.
- Create a MySpace page.
  My Space has a section specifically for film (www.myspace. com—click on *film* in the top menu bar). Through the incredible mechanism of social networking on MySpace, many filmmakers have built tremendous audiences and have gone on to secure distribution from that alone. Of course, MySpace is free, and can be done in conjunction with your own web site or blog. In other words, you don't have to make a choice between one or the other. MySpace even has a blog service of their own, so you can host your blog there if you choose to.
- Put out a press release through PRWeb.
  PRWeb (www.prweb.com) is just one of the Internet services where you can distribute your press release online to a world-wide audience. They have a free service, as well as a few upgraded options that allow for greater visibility.

  Although you may want to wait until you are actually done with production to send out a press release, it certainly can't hurt to do it while in production as well. Follow PRWeb's guidelines and use their free templates for creating effective press releases. Within twenty-four hours hours of sending out your release, you can view all the stats of how many people picked it up, viewed it, and so forth. Not a bad idea for getting the buzz going early!

- Email updates.
  This may sound obvious, but I would recommend putting out weekly production updates via email to your mailing list. If nothing else, this will keep friends and family in the loop of what you're doing. It will also keep the excitement going during production.

  Email updates can be in simple text format, or you can add links to video clips from that week's shoot. Also, add JPEG photos to the email to really give people an idea of what things look like. They'll see your film developing right before their eyes!

  One famous example of filmmakers starting publicity and buzz building during production is *The Blair Witch Project*. The filmmakers started a web site and put up daily production diaries and video clips. The project quickly caught fire, generated such interest online, and had such a massive following that by the time the movie was released, audiences flocked to theaters in droves. The film wound up grossing over $100 million at the box office. This was really the first time the Internet had been utilized in such a way. The filmmakers literally "made" a movie. Had there not been such a buzz online during production, however, it's a safe bet *The Blair Witch Project* would never have become a cultural phenomenon or grossed anything near what it ended up earning.

  Don't forget that we are now living in a much more "interactive" world. People like to immerse themselves fully in a visual experience, whether it's films, television shows, or video games. The Internet has trained us not to be passive viewers, but instead active participants. An online production diary can allow your viewers or potential viewers to immerse themselves in the production process, thus enabling them to feel a part of the making of the film.

  There is another way in which production diaries can be useful. If someone finds an interesting little quip or story included in a production diary, they may refer a friend to the site to enjoy the story as well. This means more traffic on your web site—and more traffic on your site means more viewers. Word of mouth is a very powerful tool—it can make or break a film. It's important to realize this early on and to capitalize on it fully.

Notes on distribution-focused production

from Philip Hodgetts, Managing Editor
Creative Planet's Digital Production BuZZ
(www.digitalproductionbuzz.com)

- Get a great trailer up—both on the production's web site, but also on YouTube and anywhere else that'll carry it.
- Get a MySpace page and use that to build buzz.
- Comment in the comments or forums around already-successful projects to build a little buzz for your own film—but make it genuine. For example, if a technique is being discussed, you could chime in: "We used a similar technique on *My Film's Name*, and it worked like this for us," or "We thought about using that technique, but ultimately on *My Film's Name* we used . . . ," or even "We're still working on what's best—can someone run down the differences between the technique they used here and the alternative?"
- In terms of shooting format, the standard, traditional "film" frame rate of 24 fps might just be the universal mastering format. Speed up 4 percent for 50 Hz countries; spit it out at 24 to film or cinema projection, or add pulldown for 60 Hz electronic distribution. But if you're going to plan for that, do it all the way through. Shoot progressive because it scales between sizes more accurately than interlaced footage. In other words, if you can't shoot 1080 p24, then you're better off, from a quality perspective, to shoot 720 p24 rather than 1080 interlaced at 29.97.
- Create some "making of" footage or little videos that you can put up on your web site during production, and have them for promotional collateral after production, selling a whole story around the film. Make sure the "making of" video is good enough to be used for film-promotion purposes, so near-broadcast quality at a minimum.
- Create a few "sneak preview" or "spoiler" pieces, and leak them to YouTube or one of the other sites to build buzz around the movie. Better you do than someone else does—and for maximum publicity, you could complain to the media how bad it is that your plot is being revealed (only to the extent you want it to be revealed). Or do it about some "on-set drama" or other backstory about the movie. (One situation from the movie really happened to a cast member's third cousin by marriage.)

- Create a blog and/or forum for the production. Share a little more with those who are regular users. Find where your best fans are from the blog comments (or forum comments), and treat the best fans "special." Preview the making of movies and other collateral with them before letting them release it to YouTube. Turn the enthusiasm into evangelism.
- David Lehr had one of his films posted on YouTube, and it led to a huge jump in his career—300,000 downloads the first day, more than 6 or 7 million all up. Posting video on YouTube gives you the equivalent opportunity to be discovered as the waitress in the diner in the classic Hollywood story. Big note: watch the terms and conditions of some of the online sites; they basically try and take all the rights. However, if the rights holder did not actually post the content, no rights can be transferred because the person who posted didn't have the right to pass on any rights!
- Filmmakers should set their movie up with some searches at Technorati. Membership is free, and what can be done is to create persistent searches for specified terms (as an RSS feed). So you can enter terms associated with your movie or the name of your movie, to find any comment on the subject(s) across the blogosphere.

Suggested Exercises for Part Three

1. Look at five films that have theatrical distribution right now, and notate what they were shot on and who distributed them. Also look at five straight-to-video films and what they were shot on and who distributed them. You can usually find this information by visiting the films' web sites and/or emailing the producers and asking. The purpose of this exercise is to see if distribution is in fact a function of shooting format. Write a paragraph on your findings.
2. Find five independent-film web sites with good use of film stills. Discuss how the stills are used in a way that would attract the interest of distributors.
3. Find five independent-film web sites that use production diaries, blogs, MySpace, and so on, and write a paragraph on the top two creative ways to start a buzz during production.

— 4 —

Postproduction with an Eye Toward Distribution

During postproduction is still a perfect time to begin looking for distribution. Although postproduction is associated mostly with editing, there are still a host of other things that you will need to pay attention to in regard to finding distribution. They are called deliverables.

Deliverables are the items that a distributor will require to you "deliver" as part of your distribution contract with them. I cover deliverables in greater detail later in this book, so for now I'll stay focused on postproduction deliverables.

Keep in mind that until you deliver all the items on a distributor's list, they can (and will) hold back payment to you. That is why I recommend getting these things together now, in postproduction. That way, when you get a distribution deal, you won't have to go scrambling around to get everything together, or spend unnecessary money creating things you should have done during post.

Here is a sampling of postproduction deliverables:

- M&E tracks
  Music and effects tracks (M&E) are copies of your sound mix without dialogue. These tracks allow foreign buyers to create a foreign-language dub of your film. They are done during post-sound and can be pretty costly, which is why most filmmakers avoid making an M&E track at all. However—and I cannot stress

this enough—it is a wise investment to make at this stage of the game. If you wait until later, you will have to go back and re-create the M&E track from your original audio stems, and it will end up costing you a lot more.

On several occasions, I have witnessed sales of a film fall through because there was no M&E track available, and the buyer couldn't wait the amount of time that it would take to create one. It pays to have a track made during postsound, so that when international sales are made, you are ready to deliver a master with full sound on channels 1 and 2, and M&E tracks on channels 3 and 4.

- Trailers

A trailer of your movie is important—in some cases, even more important than the film itself. Furthermore, I strongly suggest hiring an experienceed editor to cut together a trailer for you, if nothing else to have a fresh pair of eyes. A good trailer, front-loaded with action and set to good music, is the primary sales tool for your movie. At markets, there is never time to show anything more than trailers of movies—and *buyers will buy films based on the trailer*. Consequently, when I send out screening cas-settes for buyers to view, I always put the trailer at the head of the tape. That way, the buyer screening the tape can watch the trailer, get excited about the film from the outset, and then carry on watching the whole thing.

Another increasingly effective sales tool is to upload the trailer to your blog or web site. Buyers constantly go to web sites to view trailers online. It saves so much time and money—if they like the trailer and want to see more, you can send them a full screening cassette or DVD. If they don't like the trailer, you won't have to waste your time and money sending them a screening cassette, and you can move on to the next buyer.

- Music clearances

Music is often considered an afterthought in the production process. However, if you plan your songs and budget for clear-ances during the production process, you won't be caught in the scenario where you get to postproduction and realize you cannot afford the songs you want.

When a distributor buys your picture, they will assume that all the music in the movie has been cleared. Having your music sorted out ahead of time will increase your chances of getting distribution.

So how do you get the music in your film cleared? The first option is to hire a music-clearances professional. Of course, this option will depend on what budget you have left in post—most of the time, these professionals will want to be paid a fee up front. Music clearances take time and hard work. This field is a specialty unto itself. Most music-clearances professionals are adept at all the legal paperwork involved in getting written clearances. In my opinion, these pros are worth their weight in gold.

Another option is to hire a music supervisor, but music supervisors are typically hired during preproduction because they will be negotiating music rights all throughout production and into post. Music supervisors differ from music-clearances professionals because supervisors act almost as music curators for your film. Of course, you will be paying for that expertise.

Nowadays, movie soundtracks can be as popular as the films themselves, and music supervisors have been riding that wave of popularity. Creating a soundtrack album for your picture is a great way to bring added value to your project, as well as to recoup your initial investment. Many times you can sell the audio rights along with the DVD rights of your film to the same buyer, and they will release the two together. It's a value-added proposition for you *and* the buyer.

When I worked at the William Morris Agency, I started in the soundtrack department. The independent-film department would refer to us their clients who had just completed their movies. We would package the movie's songs and sell the soundtrack rights to record labels. Granted, it wasn't always a huge advance (anywhere from $10K to $25K), but the filmmaker would receive royalties, and that meant revenue down the line. Packaging songs was also excellent PR for the film. I realize that not everyone is lucky enough to have William Morris representing their project, but this is something you can certainly explore on your own or with the help of a sales rep. If you're inclined to go the do-it-yourself route, research which record labels are releasing independent-film soundtracks, then contact these companies yourself to see if there is any interest in your track listings.

The bottom line is that in order to be able to profit from a soundtrack album, or even to promote your film's soundtrack as part of the movie's appeal, you must get all your music clearances in place (in writing!) during postproduction.

• Digibeta master with certified QC report
When you do the final output of your film in post, be sure to make a clean Digibeta master and have the lab run a QC (quality check) report. I can't tell you how many distribution deals I've done that have fallen apart because the master couldn't pass the distributor's QC process.

Here's how it works: whenever you get a distribution deal for your film, whether it's domestic or foreign, the buyer (a DVD distributor or broadcast network) will put your master through their own QC process. If the master does not pass, there is no deal. Of course, you will be given the opportunity to fix what isn't up to par—for example, if the sound levels are too low—but at that point, it could cost you a lot more money than if the problem had been fixed while you were still in post.

So take the time in postproduction to run a QC report with your lab. That way, when you get a distribution deal and you deliver your film, you can attach your own QC report to show them everything is in order.

• Slides
Remember those all-important stills that I talked about in the previous chapter? Well, postproduction is a good time to go through and pick out twenty to thirty of your best action shots and put high-res formats on a disc.

The reason distributors will want action shots is because they will be creating your DVD box art with these shots, as well as posters and other publicity. That means they'll need images that can literally "sell" your movie to audiences.

A distributor's contract might require actual slides, the traditional delivery form for still images. However, CD-ROM or DVD is normally acceptable as well.

Interview with Kate Pearson, former acquisitions for HBO Latin America, and current acquisitions for the Documentary Channel

In your experience, which postproduction deliverables do most film-makers forget about?

Title treatment (which is logo artwork as opposed to a "treatment"), key art, separated audio elements—stereo; dialogue/Foley/effects/music—and, surprisingly, captioned high-resolution digital images.

Which ones are the most important for broadcast distribution?

The separated elements (for international)—making sure there is a separate M&E channel in case it needs to be dubbed into a language other than its original language. And again, the little bits and pieces like artwork, stills, logos. . . .

Is E&O (errors and omissions) insurance necessary for filmmakers to get broadcast distribution? If they don't have it when you acquire their film, will they have time to get it before signing the contract?

E&O is required for most, if not all, U.S. broadcasts. For international, it depends upon the broadcaster. Some require; some don't. There is also the matter of music rights/ASCAP. Many filmmakers forget to nail down all the legal rights and copyright aspects of their film, which can definitely be a deal breaker with a channel. The less work for the channel, the better. They like to have a filmmaker hand them as many signed, notarized legal forms as they can come up with. It's unfortunate, but it is a litigation-crazy world out there.

4. How important is a good trailer for getting broadcast distribution? Why or why not?

A good trailer is very important. Many acquisitions execs simply don't have time to watch an entire film, and if the first five minutes of a film is less than stellar, they'll often tune it out, even if it is a slow buildup to a brilliant film. A well-paced trailer will show just enough good stuff to entice the buyer to want more. Then they will watch the whole thing—or often just license the film based on the trailer and the cast and production.

What other deliverables do you feel are important to mention to filmmakers?

Scripts, music cue sheets, signed production agreements or waivers . . . any and all elements you can pull together in support of your film.

Any other advice you have to filmmakers looking for broadcast distribution?

Try to have all legal ducks in a row, and make sure all rights are covered to avoid litigation; create supporting promotional elements such as EPKs (electronic press kits), one-sheets, trailers, postcards . . . and submit the film to as many festivals as possible, because broadcasters like to see a "prior life" to a film. It gives the film legal and reputable cachet the more it is seen.

Get Objective Third-Party Feedback

I can't stress this enough: *feedback is critical!* During postproduction is the perfect time to get objective third-party feedback on your movie because you can still make changes. I recommend giving a finished cut to at least ten people in your target market, and particularly to anyone you know in the distribution field. Ask them to give you feedback on things that can be tinkered with—such as structure, look and feel, music, special effects, and editing. Then swallow your pride and take their advice seriously. This book you hold in your hands today would not be a fraction of what it is now without the relentless feedback I solicited from both filmmakers and distribution executives.

Take your notes carefully. Keep in mind, if only one person out of ten has a problem with a particular element, then it may not truly be a problem. You can't please everyone all the time. A general rule of thumb is that if three of your testers have a problem with something, then it's a real problem. In that case, a pattern has formed. Most likely, as your film is viewed by more and more people, the problem will persist and more people will pick up on it. Could they be seeing something you're not? Yes. Being the filmmaker, you are so close to the project that most of the time you cannot adequately divorce yourself from the material and look at it objectively. Your test audience can do that for you. And also remember to trust your instincts. If you have a problem with something, then it *is* a problem. If something just doesn't feel right but you don't know exactly what it is (as will be the case with a lot of filmmakers because they are so close to the material), point it out to a trusted third party or a small group of your viewers. With enough scrutiny, the problem will be found and you can fix it. Making the best picture you can is crucial to making your movie stand out from the pack—and standing out from the pack is essential to acquiring distribution.

It is even a wise investment to hire a distribution consultant at this point in the process. A distribution consultant is a professional who can give you feedback on your film strictly from a distribution perspective. Distribution consultants are often former sales agents, or sales agents moonlighting as consultants.

Using a distribution consultant in conjunction with feedback from your test audience is the best way to get an overview of how your movie is playing. If a distribution consultant points something out, however, it's in your best interest to give great weight to their advice. Their job is to tailor your picture to fit into the needs of distributors. Consultants know the market and the players, and can possibly give your film that extra fine-tuning that will translate into distributor interest.

You can find an experienced distribution consultant by word of mouth from fellow filmmakers or by looking in the classifieds sections of popular film magazines such as *Filmmaker*, *International Documentary*, or *MovieMaker*. Another way to track down a distribution consultant is through the online classifieds at Independent Feature Project (www.ifp.org).

License Stock Footage

As I mentioned previously, stock footage is an excellent tool to use during postproduction to spruce up your film and make it more attractive to distributors. I spoke before about the benefits of utilizing stock footage to make a promo or trailer to raise presale money, but now that your movie is completed, you'll want to actually go back and license those shots for your picture.

Stock footage can be used in many creative ways. For example, if you have a completed documentary, then an obvious solution to further legitimize your subject matter is to license archived news footage from reputable sources such as CNN, BBC, APTN, Reuters, and others. Think about it. If you're doing a documentary on the history of something, or a profile on someone, then wouldn't it be money well spent to license archived interviews and footage of these places or people that you obviously weren't able to get while you were shooting? Furthermore, when you are approaching distributors, it helps to say that included in your film is "licensed footage from the BBC," or whatever the case may be. This can be a huge selling point that makes or breaks distribution for your movie.

Narrative features have also discovered the value of licensing stock footage to add cachet to their production. George Clooney's 2005 film *Good Night, and Good Luck.* utilized archived CBS footage of Edward R. Murrow, which really added a whole other dimension to the movie and gave it an incredible texture.

In recent years, I have seen many narrative films that featured archived footage similar to the *Good Night, and Good Luck.* example. Another great idea is the use of stock footage to insert difficult shots that you didn't have the budget to obtain. For example, say you needed an aerial shot of Los Angeles for an establishing shot in your film. Obviously, aerial shots of cities are very expensive to get, but to license that kind of shot might cost you only a few hundred dollars. Other examples of expensive footage that is cheaper to license than to shoot: underwater footage, foreign countries/cities, other faraway places, explosions, nature shots, and so on.

If you can sprinkle enough of these valuable shots throughout your film, it can significantly add value, which of course makes your movie a more attractive product to submit to distributors.

The thing to keep in mind about licensing stock footage during postproduction is: do not license more rights than you need. For instance, if you plan to submit your picture to film festivals, start with a film-festival license. This will be much cheaper than licensing all-media, worldwide, in-perpetuity rights up front. The truth is, until you get a distributor, you don't know which rights you need to license. And unless you get a major distributor, you're not going to need all-Media, worldwide, in-perpetuity rights anyway.

So my recommendation is to play it conservative at this stage. You can always come back and upgrade your licenses later to encompass the rights you need (for example, worldwide DVD, U.S. broadcast, etc.).

Great places from which to license stock and archived footage include the following:

- BBC Motion Gallery (www.bbcmotiongallery.com)
- Getty Images (www.gettyimages.com)
- Corbis (www.corbis.com)
- ITN (www.itnsource.com)
- Thought Equity Motion (www.thoughtequity.com)
- FootageBank (www.footagebank.com)
- FOOTAGE.net (www.footage.net)

Build Your Press Kit

During postproduction is the time when you want to start building your press kit. Even though you may not have any press yet, you can still pull together other elements that will help in presentation to distributors. It is customary to submit a press kit at the same time you present a screener.

Here are the *Seven Essential Steps to Creating a Press Kit* by Elliot Grove, director of Raindance Film Festival in the United Kingdom (www.raindance.co.uk). Elliot has seen loads of press kits in his time, and I consider him an authority in this subject. Here are his seven steps:

Step 1: Create a Folder

A stationer will sell stock folders with flaps in which newspaper clippings and press releases can be organized. Press kits for ultralow budgets use stock folders from stationers with self-adhesive labels on which the name of the production company is printed. Self-adhesive labels went out with Margaret Thatcher. A better alternative is to get a professional printer to emboss the folder with the title of your film. Acquisitions executives are notoriously snobbish.

The flip side of this snobbishness is that they are easily impressed, and you would be amazed at what a little bit of gold embossing can do for your press kit.

For the low-budget press kit, you will need to buy a hundred folders. A normal film might send out a thousand or more press kits—beyond the reach of a low budget. Through skillful manipulation, you aim to create the impression that you have mailed a thousand press kits to international executives and journalists. This way, you create the impression that your film is hot.

Step 2: Write a Synopsis

A synopsis is a summary of the story of your film told in an engaging way that captures the reader's interest and makes them want to see the movie. A synopsis should never sound like ". . . and this happened, followed by this, and then this happened." This type of synopsis is certain to bore the reader. A well-written synopsis should be a teaser. There are three kinds of synopses that you should include in your press kit.

Hint: You are writing a synopsis that should sound like the paragraph on the back of the DVD or video jacket. The point of the synopsis is to make the reader want to see the movie.

i. The Long Synopsis

A single page, double spaced, in which the story is summed up in three-quarters of the page. The last three or four lines of the page contain an anecdote from the making of the movie. Ideally, this anecdote will demonstrate your incredible talent.

ii. The Medium Synopsis

Three-quarters of a page long, in which the story is summed up yet again, only more concisely. The last two or three lines are devoted to another production anecdote. Again, this anecdote will demonstrate the talent you know you have.

iii. The Short Synopsis

Half a page, with the bulk of the material devoted to a tight and punchy story summary. This is followed by another production anecdote, this time a mere one line long.

Why supply three synopses to journalists? Because you want to make it easy for them to write a review of your film. Why offer three different synopsis lengths? Because you don't yet know how much space they have in their publication. Your synopses are now ready to be photocopied.

Step 3: Write Cast and Crew Bios

You should include brief biographies of the key people you worked with on your movie. Actors' bios should include previous film roles (if any), stage work, and awards they may have won. Key crew bios (such as those for your director of photography, production designer, editor, and composer) should detail other directors they have worked for and other productions they have worked on, or other relevant experience., For example my DP shot a commercial for Burger King, and my production designer created a table for IKEA.

Be certain that you have a brief, concise, and interesting biography for yourself. If this is your first film project and you have absolutely no other movie experience, then you could include any previous work. For example, Elliot Grove, an ex-carpenter, produced his first feature film using project-management and organizational skills he learned on building sites. If your previous work experience, like mine, sounds too lame to be of interest, you might simply list your education credits. Your total cast and crew bios should run to no more than three or four pages. When photocopied, these pages should be stapled together to keep them separate from the synopses.

Step 4: Create Ten FAQs

Creating hype and publicity for your movie means that you have to give precise direction and guidance to the people who hear about your picture: film-festival programmers, film journalists, and, of course, acquisition executives. I was in London during the launch of Quentin Tarantino's *Reservoir Dogs,* and was fortunate enough to see his press kit. Scanning it reassured me that Tarantino was not relying on the judgment of film critics—or even of the moviegoing public—to determine that he was an amazingly talented filmmaker. He was printing this judgment himself in his press kit, under the guise of the "Ten Most Frequently Asked Questions of Quentin Tarantino During the Making of *Reservoir Dogs.*" Immediately following the questions were printed his answers.

Hint: Film hype is not earned. It is manufactured by you. It is you who have the power to turn yourself into a cult filmmaker, and your picture into a cult movie.

Doing this for yourself will be an easy thing to complete, because the ten questions will be the same ten questions that everyone has been asking you during the making of your picture. On my film, the questions included the following: What was it like working with nonprofessional actors? If you had to do it over again, what would you do differently? What did you learn about directing films? How did you get the notorious "Mad" Frankie Fraser to star in your film? Who are your influences? Where do you see the future of British filmmaking?

List your ten questions on a page, and after each question type an answer about five lines long. You are hoping that a journalist will be intrigued by your film, but for whatever reason will be unable to reach you in time for their press deadline. If this happens, then the journalist could write: "Contacted today from New York, Elliot Grove said. . . ." By listing these questions and answers, you are also giving the journalist a taste of how you will react to similar questions—and accordingly, how you will appeal to the readership of the particular publication.

Step 5: Get Publicity Stills

Although your press kit has a slick, glossy cover, three synopses, cast and crew bios, and FAQs, you still need to have photographs. Getting a good publicity still is a true art form. The right still can be used on the poster, in newspaper ads, on video and DVD covers, on T-shirts—in fact, everywhere your movie is mentioned. Truly memorable images, such as the eyes from *The Blair Witch Project,* cross into popular culture and are mimicked and satirized by others.

Publicity stills that work are photographs that include action. The stills photographer you hire should have a portfolio of stills that demonstrate movement and action within the frame. Ask the photographer to attend the shoot on the day that the most action is happening. Perhaps it is the day with the dueling swordsmen, or the pistol shot, or the day you managed to get a large crane onto the set. The photographer needs to take four kinds of stills:

1. Stills of the cast reenacting key moments of the movie. The photographer cannot click away during the shoot because the microphones will pick up the shutter noise. After a suitable take, ask the actors to hold their marks. You can then rearrange the actors to suit the frame, and get the photographer to capture the moment for posterity.

2. Stills of the cast and crew showing off the production values of the picture: show as much film equipment as you can, show the fake head being glued onto the actor, the fingernails being ripped off, whatever—but make sure it contains loads of action. Journalists and the public all concur that a picture tells a thousand words.

3. Get pictures of yourself producing. If nothing else, you will want a record of your efforts to prove that you actually produced a movie. But photos of a person producing a film are pretty lame: generally they are shots of someone reading a script or signing a check. In order to make the photos of yourself more dramatic, turn to the theater and use a stage trick employed by accomplished actors when they are onstage with other actors and wish to show them up. The trick is to pull out your finger and point. Try it. Look at some photographs of filmmakers, and they are invariably pointing. Take your stills photographer to the set and tell him or her that everytime you point, you want to hear the shutter go. You can point at anything—a speck of

fluff on someone's jacket, the sun, your foot . . . you can even point at your nose. It doesn't matter. Point, then make sure you hear the click of the camera. In actual fact, there are really only two times that you point when you are on the set as a producer. The first is when you say, "You, with the attitude—you're fired. Off the set. Now." And the second is "Thank you for sharing that with me." Whereupon you will usually wander off to watch a movie for an hour or two until things cool down.

4. Photos of yourself with celebrities. Even if you do not have a star working on the film, try and convince a local celebrity to attend your set, again on a day with a lot of action. When they show up, give them a polite tour of your set, introduce them to the key people on the crew, and allow them time to ask questions. For many, this will be the first time they have been on a film set, and your low-budget shoot may not fall into their preconceived ideas of what a film set should like. At the appropriate moment, politely ask your invited celebrity if you could have a picture or two with them. If necessary, offer to send them a copy. When you are ready, make sure that you are standing stage right (camera left). And point!

Hint: Always stand stage right to have your picture taken. Why? Captions run left to right, and this position guarantees that your name will appear first. If you start studying the publicity stills used by successful film people, you will see that they follow these rules.

Step 6: Include Reviews and Third-Party Endorsements

Third-party endorsements always work wonders in the world of promotion. All commercial enterprises use third-party endorsements. You may use toothpaste recommended by the British Dental Association, eat a certain breakfast cereal on the recommendation of a leading nutritionist, and see a movie because a certain journalist—probably well known for their taste and judgment—has put a film onto their own must-see list.

By getting a journalist to see and review your picture, you are starting to create buzz for your film. Make a copy of the review and include it in your press kit. Even if the journalist disliked your movie, the review they print will most likely include a superlative somewhere in the opening one or two sentences. Film journalists have careers too. They want to be quoted and have their name splashed on the poster. If they didn't like the picture but still include a superlative in their review, they know that you will quote them out of context. So "an amazingly inept first film" becomes "an amazing first film." When you print the reviewer's name and publication after the quote, you are helping their name awareness. Journalists are always trying to increase their stature among the readership, or striving to get a better job. With your poster in their portfolio, their reputation is enhanced, and they have an even better chance of moving their career upward. Essentially, you are helping each other.

Journalists and Film Festivals

Critics have a love-hate relationship with film festivals. On one hand, they enjoy and thrive in the glamorous atmosphere of a festival. If the right filmmakers are in attendance, the journalists will be able to do many interviews in a short space of time. They can then warehouse these interviews until needed. What reviewers dislike about film festivals is the fact that they have to watch movies—and lots of them. Usually they screen these films alone at home from cassette. Few festivals have the resources to show the films ahead of time at private screenings for journalists. Suppose that you have entered a small regional festival in Europe or the United States in a town or small city that has a weekly community paper. This paper will have an entertainment section devoted to printing the press kits and photographs of films released by the distributors in the area. The entertainment editor probably has another area to cover as well: perhaps it is sports or travel. When the local film festival arrives, this journalist will be asked to cover the festival and preview all the films. When they reach your film, they discover that your press kit has three synopses: long, medium and short. The reviewer knows that their work will be made easier by this simple addition to your press kit. Next, they discover the cast and crew bios, which are short and succinct.

Finally, they see the ten FAQs. Now they can watch the film, make notes, and know they have ample information on which to base their review. And even if they hated your film, they will be able to write an intelligent article based on the information you have provided. Critics tend to include a superlative in the review of a film they dislike, because they know you will quote them out of context. For example: "Elliot Grove's first film was an extraordinary example of incompetence." The quote out of context would become: "Elliot Grove's first film was extraordinary." Reviewers want to be quoted, they want a big line printed on your poster, and they want their name printed underneath the quote. They are hoping to get a job on that city's daily paper, or maybe move to a national paper or magazine.

Step 7: Create an Electronic Press Kit

An electronic press kit (EPK) is a set of videos and CD-ROMs with photos and interviews with the principal cast and crew. The EPK is duplicated and distributed to appropriate people. This is difficult to accomplish on a low budget.

During the shoot, hire a documentary filmmaker to take high-quality video footage. Include interviews with the key actors, the director, the producer, and other principal crew where appropriate. For example, if your movie features prosthetic heads being lopped off, interview the prop maker and the special-effects artists. You are looking for angles that might help you sell the story of the film later.

When doing interviews, have someone ask key people on the cast and crew questions from your ten FAQs. Then film the answers. If possible, set up some of the interviews in front of a simple cloth or curtain with a poster behind the interviewee. In this way, you can deliver the interview to a television station and they can cut in their own reviewer, making it look like they were in the same room, when in actual fact they have never met. You should make VHS copies as well as Digibeta copies (for television). The tape can also include a short trailer for the movie.

Broadcasters welcome EPKs because they represent free content. You will have to guarantee to any television station that the music rights are cleared for broadcast.

Suggested Exercises for Part Four

1. Post the links to a good trailer and a bad trailer. Explain why each works or doesn't work in attracting distributors.
2. Talk with a sound designer about M&E tracks. Write a paragraph on your findings on what needs to be done during postproduction to create your M&E tracks, dos and don'ts, and how much money to set aside for them. Also find out how much it will cost you later in time and money if you don't create M&E tracks in the first place.
3. Research five songs you want to use in your movie. List the publishers and the record companies. Call them to get quotes for (1) DVD rights only, (2) all rights, and (3) festival-only rights.

— 5 —

It's in the Can—Now What?

Once you've completed your film, you're now at the stage where you'll start getting anxious to find distribution. You've put in all this hard work, and it's time to get your movie out there and find its audience.

Many filmmakers' instinct once they have a finished product is to immediately start shopping it to every distributor in sight. However, this is not an effective approach. I would advise taking a more methodical approach to finding distribution for your film, which I'll outline below.

For example, the first thing you want to do before you even start approaching anyone to distribute or represent your picture is to get your campaign together. You don't want to be haphazardly submitting items to distributors and reps without taking into account any type of protocol.

How to Create a Campaign

Many filmmakers forget that they don't market to the general public; rather, they market to distributors! When marketing your picture to sales reps and distributors, presentation is everything. Once your movie is actually acquired by a distributor, they will create their own marketing campaign. However, in the meantime, it is your job to market your film *to* them. Creating your own campaign is perhaps the most important job at this point.

It's important to start by hiring a graphic designer to create marketable cover art for your movie. Make sure you save the cover art in "layered" Photoshop files. You can use this to make a one-sheet/flyer, and to put on your DVD before you submit to potential distributors. Also have the graphic designer build a web page for you. If you already have a web site from production, go ahead and update it with your new "campaign." Be sure to include a synopsis and a trailer of the film on your web site as well. These are all very valuable tools to have so that buyers from all over the world can access your site, check out your campaign, and view your trailer.

Here are some good examples of independent-film campaigns I've come across:

www.thefunkparlor.com
www.thetwomillion.com
www.stbp.com
www.tropixthemovie.com

Applying to Film Festivals: Your Strategy

After creating a campaign, you are now ready to tackle film-festival submissions. My theory is that there are a small handful of festivals that are considered the prestigious ones. Should you get your project accepted to one of these, your chances of distribution are that much better. There are also hundreds of smaller film festivals to which you can submit your picture. Even if distributors don't attend these smaller festivals, showing your movie there can still be good exposure. Any chance to garner awards for your film or get local press/reviews can be an asset to your overall campaign and your press kit.

The film-festival strategy that I personally recommend is to have a Plan A and Plan B in place. Here's how it works.

Plan A is to apply to Tier 1 festivals first: Toronto, Sundance, Cannes, Berlin, Los Angeles, SXSW, AFI FEST, and Tribeca. What makes these festivals Tier 1? The fact that they are the ones that most distributors will attend is reason enough for you target them first. If your ultimate goal is to get distribution for your picture, then wouldn't you want to be at festivals where the distributors go? Of course you would!

My advice is to take an honest look at your picture and listen to the feedback you get from third parties. If you think your movie is up to par for getting into one of these top festivals, by all means apply to them all. Keep in mind, however, that most of these festivals will require a worldwide or North American premiere—which means if you accept an invitation to one festival, you cannot premiere your film in any of the others. For this reason, it is imperative to check the rules and regulations of the festivals you are interested in. That is another reason why I say that you should apply to the big festivals first. If you happen to prematurely accept an offer from a smaller festival, then you automatically disqualify your movie from premiering in one of the top-tier festivals. Wouldn't you kick yourself if, after you had already accepted an invitation to some small festival, Sundance were to come calling and you had to decline?

Speaking of Sundance, the other thing to keep in mind is that with Sundance in particular, many movies that are accepted are picked way in advance and already have distribution deals in place. In other words, oftentimes distributors will make a deal with Sundance to premiere a film there without the film's having to go through the normal submissions process. This, of course, means even less of a chance that your picture will get accepted, simply because there are so few spots available for actual independent films.

The good news in all this is that in most big festivals, there are both competitive and noncompetitive categories, so even if your project is not a world premiere, it may still be submitted as a non-compete entry. And even if your picture gets accepted as a non-compete, you will still benefit from the exposure of being at one of the big festivals.

When applying to the top-tier festivals, submit your application and then just sit tight. I know that waiting can get nerve-racking, and you'll be tempted to go on a festival-application spree, but remember: the mere chance of getting into one of these top festivals is worth the wait. It can be the difference between getting distribution and not getting distribution.

Wherever you decide to premiere your film will be considered your launch festival. Just remember to choose it carefully.

What if Plan A fails? What if either you honestly don't think your movie is up to par for one of the top-tier festivals, or you apply to them all and don't get accepted to any? Then it's time to invoke Plan B.

Plan B is to submit your film to the many Tier 2 festivals out there. Tier 2 festivals include Palm Springs, Santa Barbara, Chicago International, Austin, Hamptons, and CineVegas. This is by no means an exhaustive list. I recommend checking in with the online festival-submitting service Withoutabox (www.withoutabox.com) for the definitive list of festivals out there. In general, anything in or near major cities is a good bet because there might be a chance that one or two distributors will be present (especially if the festival is near New York or L.A., where most distributors are located).

When applying to second-tier festivals, it's O.K. to cast a wide net. These festivals most likely will not require a world premiere the way the first-tier festivals do. Your strategy, once you get to any of these festivals, should be to get as much press as possible. Even if there aren't any distributors present to see your film on the big screen, you can at least work on building up your press kit. That way, when you do start submitting to distributors and reps, you'll have some favorable press to show them. A good press kit goes a long way in attracting a distributor's attention.

Some people ask how exactly to go about getting press at a film festival. Whether you've been accepted to a first-tier or second-tier festival, I definitely recommend hiring a publicist who specializes in independent films. You should do this at least one or two months prior to the festival—the more lead time, the better. A publicist will be very adept at writing a press release and getting it into the hands of the right journalists so that they will come and cover your movie.

Interview with PR specialist Alexia Haidos, Double A PR

(www.doublea-pr.com): *The Ice Cream Man, A Taxi Odyssey, Eating*

Alexia, why is it important to have a PR specialist on board if you get accepted into one of the big film festivals? Can it help attract distributors?

I highly recommend bringing a publicist on board when your film has been accepted into a big festival. An effective public relations strategy will increase awareness about your film. A publicist knows how to create a buzz about the film by garnering press coverage through the creation of effective press materials and through follow-up and contacts at a variety of outlets such as television, newspapers, magazines, radio, Internet, and other media.

It's a delicate balance. It's important to get media attention during the festival, but it's also important that the film is not heavily reviewed during this time—because reviews in certain outlets might only happen once, and it is essential that they happen when the film is released theatrically.

If a filmmaker doesn't get accepted into any of the *big* film festivals, can a good PR campaign still help attract distributors outside of the festival circuit? What's a good example of this?

Smaller festivals are still on the map with distributors. Aside from festivals, media coverage is essential to raise a project's visibility to distributors.

What are your thoughts on some of the smaller film festivals, and what can be done in those markets?

The smaller festivals are still festivals, and are a press-worthy event in the local media venues. Often there is not much lead time from the festival acceptance letter to the time of the screening. This is why it is a good idea to have press materials and images available about your film. Press materials can be sent directly to the journalists covering the festival locally; this is a great way to be included in an overview article about the festival.

Make sure to have your press materials, including easy-to-download images up on your web site, available to the press. Making the journalists' job as easy as possible can really make a difference in getting the film covered by the media. Hometown newspapers of the filmmakers should also be approached.

Postcards and posters should be distributed throughout the city hosting the festival; an event can be created, too, to create more awareness. With the short film The Ice Cream Man, *we had an ice cream truck come to each screening, and free ice cream was given out to those attending the film. The key is to create word of mouth wherever the film goes.*

In terms of an overall PR/marketing plan, do you recommend a multitude of platforms such as the web, print, postcards, and parties/events? What's been one of your favorite or most successful campaigns in terms of raising awareness for a film and ultimately attracting a distributor?

An overall PR/marketing plan is highly recommended. The Internet is one of the most effective tools for indie filmmakers. Have a web site up from the time you begin preproduction, and use email to get the word out. A grassroots approach that includes a multitude of platforms is highly recommended. This includes the web, postcards, posters, a public relations strategy, and other promotional tie-ins. Think outside the box. Many effective campaigns have been created on a shoestring budget. Be smart, clever, and creative.

Finding Producer Reps and Sales Agents

While waiting to hear back from film festivals, it's a good time to start researching reputable producer reps and sales agents. Sometimes filmmakers will sign on with producer reps or sales agents prior to going on the festival circuit, and sometimes they will wait and find representation while attending one of the festivals. My suggestion is the following: while meeting with reps and agents during the film-festival application process, you might come across one that is crazy about your project and who wants to work with you on launching your movie at a festival and on coming up with a distribution strategy. If it really clicks for you, then go ahead and sign on with them. Alternatively, if all the reps and agents you are meeting during this period seem not quite up to par with what you had in mind, with no real strategy for your picture to speak of, then it's best to wait until you're actually at the film festivals themselves, because there you may get approached by reps and agents better suited to your project—someone who can appreciate your film more now that it is showing at a festival.

Many filmmakers ask what the actual difference is between a producer rep and a sales agent. Technically, they are the same thing. The argument can be made, however, that a producer rep takes a greater interest in a filmmaker's long-term career goals. For example, whereas a sales agent is solely responsible for getting distribution deals for your movie, a producer rep will guide you to choosing the right launch festival for your film and making sure all the right people attend your screening. Although producer reps generally do not specialize in foreign sales, often they will help the filmmaker find a reputable foreign-sales agent to take over those duties.

Historically, most distributors have said that films represented by a producer rep or sales agent have a certain cachet over unrepresented films. However, with today's technology, and with self-distribution more of a real option then ever before, the general attitude of distributors is starting to change. Granted, pictures that are represented by high-end sales agencies and producer reps will always have a certain cachet, but only a few of these top-tier companies have that kind of sway. So, for 90 percent of the independent films out there, it doesn't make that much of a difference to distributors whether you are represented or not.

One benefit of working with a rep or sales agent is that they work on commission. This means that it is always in their best interest to get the highest price for your film per territory. Furthermore, reps may be able to squeeze more revenue out of a movie by splitting up rights. For example, splitting up cable, DVD, and theatrical rights rather than doing an all-media deal can mean more money down the line for the producer. A producer may unknowingly sign away all rights—cable, DVD, and theatrical—in an all-media package. The result is far less money than he or she could get by selling the rights separately.

In some cases, distributors may prefer to deal with experienced salespeople rather than with producers themselves. Think about it. Filmmakers may not always know the nitty-gritty details of negotiating distribution contracts. Distributors realize this, and are often more willing to play ball with an agent or rep, rather then go through the hassle of having to educate an unrepresented producer about how to negotiate their own distribution contract. This is also why some producers can get taken to the cleaners by distributors—they just may not know the intricate details of distribution contracts, and therefore not get the best possible deal. Bottom line: you need someone on your side whose business it is to know these things.

In my experience, producer reps and sales reps charge fees of anywhere between 10 and 25 percent per distribution deal, depending on how much overhead they have. If the reps have big-company overhead, they will charge closer to 25 percent. If you can find a good independent producer rep or sales agent, they will charge closer to the 10 percent fee because the independents don't have the huge overheads and operating costs of bigger sales companies. With independents, you will most likely be responsible for making all your own dubs, shipping out screening cassettes to buyers on your dime, and covering all the costs of printing up flyers and other marketing materials.

A reputable sales agent should not charge you any fees up front; rather, it is customary that they will take their distribution fee off the top of every sale they make. Furthermore, if you are dealing with a big agency, keep in mind that they bear the cost of marketing your film to distributors, and therefore they share in the financial risk. In this way, the sales company is motivated to sell your film and recoup their initial investment. Agents and reps have long-term established relationships with various buyers, and these relationships can make a difference in securing a sale.

Selling films is a specialized business that requires comprehensive knowledge of distribution and market trends. Producers who try and make their own sales (particularly international sales) could find they've bitten off more than they can chew.

The best way to find producer reps and sales agents is by attending film festivals and getting word-of-mouth recommendations. Producer reps and sales agents will be representing their pictures and actively recruiting new clients at film festivals, so this may give you a chance to get an introduction and see them in action right then and there. For another great word-of-mouth resource for getting recommendations on agents and reps, check out Internet message boards.

When Searching for Reputable Reps and Foreign-Sales Agents, You should Follow these Five Steps

1. Ask around to see what their reputation is. Ask the rep for references from other producers, and be sure to call and check their references. If a rep refuses to provide references or gives you the runaround, this is generally a red flag that their reputation may be less than stellar or they may have something to hide. In this case, move on and find a rep who will gladly stand by the work they've done and their track record.
2. Look at their catalog and the other projects they're selling to see if yours fits in.
3. Remember that producer reps are adept at getting you a U.S. deal, so it's still necessary to get a foreign-sales agent.
4. Look at what their success rate has been in selling movies.
5. Sit down with your potential rep and ask questions about what territories they think they can sell your film in. Try to take several meetings and choose wisely. Decide who will work best for you and your film.

And remember, bigger isn't always better. For some, a larger sales agency is a good fit, especially if you've been doing this for a while and have an established reputation. Larger agencies have big catalogs and can leverage their might. They can also wrap several films around one really sought-after property. Meaning: if an agent or rep is representing a picture that distributors are clamoring for, the agent or rep can often make the sale contingent on the distributor's buying several other movies in their catalog as well. It's basically selling several flicks as a package deal.

Smaller reps can't wield this card. Nonetheless, for many filmmakers, especially those just starting out, the smaller rep may be the better option. The fact that the larger agencies have such extensive catalogs is as much a curse as it is a blessing, because filmmakers can often get lost in the shuffle. Smaller reps may have the same contacts as bigger reps, and will most likely give your film more individualized attention than someone with a huge slate. It is also in the best interest of the smaller rep to not let your film fall by the wayside—their livelihood depends on your project's selling for as much as possible. Sometimes young and hungry is the best and most effective way to go.

Additional Tips to Keep in Mind

- Have measured expectations
  Don't expect to make back your investors' money through foreign sales alone. Count on recouping your money through a U.S. deal, and let the foreign sales be icing on the cake.

     Nine times out of ten, filmmakers will not see any money from foreign sales. This is because the sales agencies typically have to recoup their marketing costs *first*, before they pay out to filmmakers. And with international prices at an all-time low, sales agencies rarely recoup the marketing expenses for independent films, and therefore rarely pay out to filmmakers.
- Negotiate distribution fees and marketing expenses
  As I stated previously, most sales agencies charge a 25 percent "off-the-top" distribution fee for sales they make on your picture. In addition, they will want to keep the first $30K to $50K in sales of your film, and claim that money as "marketing expenses." In all fairness, I will say that a lot of money is expended in marketing films through artwork, flyers, shipping, dubbing, and the international markets and trade shows.

     My suggestion is to try and negotiate these marketing caps in advance, and either ask for a lower cap (say, $10K), or try for a straight 30 percent distribution fee with no recoupment of expenses. This would mean that for every sale the agency makes, they take their 30 percent distribution fee and send you the balance. In other words, you would start getting paid from dollar one, instead of after marketing expenses are recouped. It means a little less money for you in the short run, but at least you'll be getting paid something.

- Use a collection account

  In your contract with the foreign-sales agency, you can always include a clause stating that when sales of your film are made, proceeds will go to a collection account. A collection account is an independent third party that provides filmmakers full insight into the financial status of a project, as well as protection against default and fraudulent behavior (e.g., failure of the foreign-sales agency to disclose actual sales made and/or failure in paying out proceeds from sales).

  Ask your local bank about setting up a collection account. You can more easily learn the details and ins and outs from a financial institution.

Sales Agencies to Consider

The Big Agencies

When I did a survey of my buyers to ask from whom they purchased most of their films, the big agencies are the ones that appeared most often on the list. They are top-tier foreign-sales agencies selling regularly to the larger television networks and DVD companies around the world. Most of the time, they will "find" you, rather than your "finding" them—meaning that the big agencies get most of their properties by acquiring them at the major film festivals, or through referrals by U.S. theatrical distributors or talent agencies, rather than through submissions by filmmakers.

The upside of these companies is that if they choose to represent your project, you are almost guaranteed sales around the world. The downside is that unless you have a picture with at least one A-list star attached, they won't take you on.

Wild Bunch
 99, rue de la Verrerie
 75004 Paris
 France
 T: (33) 1 53 01 50 20
 F: (33) 1 53 01 50 49
 231 Portobello Road

London W11 1LT
United Kingdom
T: (44) 20 7792 9791
F: (44) 20 7792 9871
www.wildbunch.biz

Fortissimo Films
Veemarkt 77–79
1019 Amsterdam PA
Netherlands
T: (31) 20 627 3215
F: (31) 20 626 1155
www.fortissimofilms.com

Pathé Distribution
10, rue Linclon
75008 Paris
France
T: (33) 01 40 76 91 69
F: (33) 01 40 76 91 94
www.patheinternational.fr

Celluloid Dreams
2, rue Turgot
75009 Paris
France
T: (33) 01 49 70 03 70
F: (33) 01 49 70 03 71
www.celluloid-dreams.com

Fireworks International
Tennyson House
159–165 Great Portland Street
London W1W 5PA
United Kingdom
T: (44) 20 7307 6300
F: (44) 20 7307 6399
www.fireworksentertainment.com

Myriad Pictures
1520 D Cloverfield Boulevard
Santa Monica, CA 90404

USA
T: (1) 310 279 4000
F: (1) 310 279 4001
www.myriadpictures.com

Moviehouse Entertainment
9 Grafton Mews
London W1T 5HZ
United Kingdom
T: (44) 20 7380 3999
F: (44) 20 7380 3998
www.moviehouseent.com

Arclight Films
9229 Sunset Boulevard
Suite 705
Los Angeles, CA 90069
USA
T: 310 777 8855
www.arclightfilms.com

Midsize and Boutique Agencies

The following midsize and boutique agencies might be interested in your picture if it is completed or if you are currently in production. Although they would prefer that you have a star or two attached, I have seen midsize and boutique agencies selling movies without any stars attached. In this case, you should definitely have your campaign prepared before approaching these agencies. You need to show them that you have your act together and are serious and committed to doing what it takes to get your film in front of audiences.

Dream Entertainment
8489 West 3rd Street
Suite 1038
Los Angeles, CA 90048
USA
T: (1) 323 655 5501

F: (1) 323 655 5603

www.dreamentertainment.net

Showcase Entertainment

21800 Oxnard Street

Suite 150

Woodland Hills, CA 91367

USA

T: (1) 818 715 7005

F: (1) 818 715 7009

www.showcasentertainment.com

MarVista Entertainment

12519 Venice Boulevard

Los Angeles, CA 90066

USA

T: (1) 310 737 0950

F: (1) 310 737 9115

www.marvista.net

Echelon Entertainment

400 South Victory Boulevard

Suite 203

Burbank, CA 90028

USA

T: (1) 818 558 1820

F: (1) 818 558 1877

www.echelonent.com

Vision Films

4626 Lemona Avenue

Sherman Oaks, CA 91403

USA

T: (1) 818 784 1702

F: (1) 818 788 3715

www.visionfilms.net

First Look International

8000 Sunset Boulevard

East Penthouse

Los Angeles, CA 90046

USA

T: (1) 323 337 1000
F: (1) 323 337 1037
www.firstlookmedia.com

Harmony Gold USA
7655 Sunset Boulevard
Los Angeles, CA 90046
USA
T: (1) 323 851 4900
F: (1) 323 851 5599
www.harmonygold.com

Mainline Releasing
Lightning Entertainment
301 Arizona Avenue
Suite 400—Penthouse
Santa Monica, CA 90401
USA
T: (1) 310 255 1200
F: (1) 310 255 1202
www.mainlinereleasing.com

PorchLight Entertainment
11777 Mississippi Avenue
Los Angeles, CA 90025
USA
T: (1) 310 477 8400
F: (1) 310 477 5555
www.porchlight.com

Sandra Carter Global
43-32 22nd Street
Room 300
Long Island City, NY 11101
USA
T: (1) 718 752 9252
F: (1) 718 752 9256
www.sandra-carter.com

Solid Entertainment
601 Santa Monica Boulevard
Suite 201

Santa Monica, CA 90401
USA
T: (1) 310 319 3440
F: (1) 310 319 3442
www.solidentertainment.com

TvFilmBiz Int'l
20501 Ventura Boulevard
Suite 210
Woodland Hills, CA 91364
USA
www.tvfilmbiz.com

Filmmaker Case Study: Percy Angress, in His Own Words

Having crawled through the no-man's-land of indie film distribution, we've learned a few lessons. The four most important are:

1. *Get a name.*
2. *Get a name.*
3. *Get a name.*
4. *Make sure your movie's subject and tone are "indie." If your script could have been a studio film, you'll have a harder time finding distribution. Audiences go to indie films for "something different," not a cheaper version of what they can get from DreamWorks for the same ticket price.*

When we were searching for a distributor, we found the first, last, and often only, question asked was not "What's it about?" "How do audiences respond?" or "Who's your target audience?" . . . but "Who's in it?" The reason, we soon learned, was not simplistic, crass, commercial distributor mind-sets (though I won't rule these out), but the understandable consideration that in the absence of, say, a "Best Picture" award from Sundance, the best—and often only—advertising "hook" distributors have for a film (and therefore the best chance of recouping their marketing investment) is the familiarity of the actors. (And be honest. Don't you often ask, when you hear of a new movie, "Who's in it?")

After consulting with industry professionals, we decided to begin our search with a foreign-film agent rather than a domestic distributor. We were advised, "You can have an L.A. screening for domestic distributors, but in that case you'll be placing all your chips on the red. If the screening doesn't wow them, word will travel fast, and your film will be D.O.A. On the other hand, foreign-film agents don't tend to talk to each other. If one doesn't respond to your screener, the next one may. Then, after you get some foreign distribution, you can work backward— try to line up a domestic distributor on the strength of your foreign sales."

We chose this strategy, and it worked for us. Ironically, our agency immediately landed U.S. DVD distribution, and only later foreign. We have since advised filmmakers seeking domestic (versus theatrical) DVD distribution to try approaching domestic DVD distributors directly via a query letter. If successful, this cuts out the agency middleman. (But consult a lawyer before signing!)

Our representation campaign took a month. We sent query letters and poster art to foreign-film agencies, then screeners to all who were interested. In the end, we had six companies asking to handle our film. We met with them all, and narrowed it down to two—one more established, the other energetically up-and-coming but without much track record. We signed with the larger, considering them the safer bet, but we remain curious how the smaller would have performed.

When making this choice, I strongly advise producers to:

- *Judge the people as best you can, then go with those you trust. Companies* are *their people.*
- *Ask for references from their current and past clients. If these aren't provided, consider it a warning sign.*
- *In any case, call other producers represented by the company and ask, privately, for their assessement. A good company will have happy clients.*
- *Get a trusted lawyer to review and negotiate the contract. This is especially important in the event you are initially handed a "dummy contract."*
- *Subsequently, hold your distributor or foreign-sales agency accountable to the contract. Some consider it a list of suggestions. It's not.*

- *In case of a disagreement, never lose your cool, put everything in writing, and don't back down. Power and money are about the only two values anyone in Hollywood respects.*

Distribution is the realm in which indie filmmakers tend to have least experience, and sometimes least interest. Yet it is as important to the success of your movie as any other stage. Take it seriously, do your home-work, and stay vigilant.

A final piece of fundamental advice for filmmakers: don't do anything until you have a good script. Everything flows from the screenplay. It must be tight, complete, and polished before you shoot. It should be vetted by an experienced writer or script analyst. I can't count the times I've seen a beautifully shot, wonderfully acted, edgy, interesting indie . . . with a flabby script, two-act structure, wooden dialogue, flat ending, or all of the above. Conversely, analyze the script of most any breakout indie, and you'll find an elegant, solid, well-structured story. The bard had it right: the play's the thing.

Navigating International Film Markets

International film markets are where producer reps and sales agents take their slate of pictures to sell to distributors. Film markets differ from film festivals in that markets are essentially big trade shows for buyers and sellers of movies, whereas festivals are more of a showcase and competition. Also, although U.S. distributors attend the big film festivals I outlined in the previous section, interna-tional distributors in general do not attend festivals. To buy the rights to the movies they want, they wait for the film markets. Film markets are essential for independent pictures because, unlike studio movies that have output deals in every foreign territory, independent films must be sold territory by territory.

Film markets are set up like this: sales agencies and production. Companies will purchase space to set up their "booths" (i.e., their little piece of real estate) at the market. The booth contains posters and other sales tools for the pictures that these companies are rep-resenting. Sellers make appointments with buyers in advance, and carry on meetings at the booth, every hour on the hour for the duration of the market. Markets typically last anywhere from five to ten days.

During a buyer's appointment at a seller's booth, the seller will screen several trailers of appropriate films, depending on the type of buyer. For example, if meeting with a Thai DVD buyer, the seller will be sure to screen all the action- and horror-flick trailers that they have in their slate. If meeting with a broadcast buyer who is interested in nonfiction programming, the seller will screen their documentary trailers.

Oftentimes, distributors will commit to buying a film on the spot, especially if they don't want their competitors to have it. In this case, the buyer and seller negotiate prices and terms right there at the booth, and sign a deal memo to confirm the agreement. Once the market is over, it is the seller's responsibility to take all the deal memos they signed at the market and draft formal contracts for the deals, then follow up with the buyer for signature and payment.

Filmmakers often ask me if it is in their best interest to attend film markets. My answer is twofold.

One, if your film is currently being represented at the market by an agent or rep, then no, it does not make sense for you to attend. Why? Because most likely the sales agent will want to stay focused on selling your picture and will not want you in the way. Plus, if your movie is being represented there anyway, it will only make you nervous to be there—wondering if any sales are being made on your film, and knowing there's nothing you can do about it one way or another. In fact, it is best to wait until a couple weeks after the market to get an update from your rep.

Two, if your film is not currently being represented at the market by an agent or rep, then it could be advantageous for you to attend the market simply as an observer. It can be beneficial to walk around to the different booths and take notes on which companies are selling which types of films. You can then approach these companies after the market about possibly representing your project. Do not approach these companies to represent your movie at the actual market. Companies are there for one reason only: to sell films. And they spend an enormous amount of money to be there.

Therefore, they will not take kindly to being approached by film-makers for representation.

The key film markets to keep in mind are:

- Cannes, Marché du Film: held simultaneously with the Cannes Film Festival
- American Film Market (AFM): held simultaneously with the AFI FEST in Los Angeles
- MIPCOM: in Cannes and geared toward DVD and broadcast buyers
- Toronto: held simultaneously with the Toronto International Film Festival
- Hong Kong, FILMART: geared toward Asian buyers
- DISCOP: held in Budapest and geared toward Central and Eastern European buyers

You will notice that some of the film markets are actually held in conjunction with film festivals. This is because if a movie is accepted into a film festival such as Cannes, it allows distributors from all over the world not only to view the movie at a proper screening, but to bid on it right then and there.

A Film-Market Prep Guide

Here are some firsthand experiences from filmmakers who went to the American Film Market on their own.

From Glenn H.:
While I don't know how beneficial the market would be for someone looking for funding for a new project, it was very beneficial for us (with one fully funded in post right now). While we were not prepared to show a screener, we were able to make a high-level sales pitch that went very well in most cases. I was surprised at how receptive the distributors were to meeting with us. We emailed, mailed, and faxed about sixty companies prior to the meeting to set up meetings for later in the week (after the buyers had made their rounds for the most part), then went in for a quick "meet and greet" with them while there. I was very happy with the response we received from the companies we spoke with. AFM proved

an invaluable opportunity to get face time with these companies, so that when we complete post and send in our screeners, we already have a relationship.

From Tiffany G.:
This year's AFM was my first time attending it. I had a booth on the second floor, selling only one feature film—*Deceitfully Funny*, a romantic comedy—and promoting two development projects. I didn't expect any success out of it because I knew my low-budget feature with no-name actors was hard to sell. Plus, my development projects were a no-deal either, since presale seems to be a nonexistence. However, one of my development projects was a big hit of interest from a lot of companies if it were to be shot and done. Even though I didn't have any deals, I've learned a lot about the demand of the market. I would love to learn more how other filmmakers get their development projects financed and distributed.

From Linda N.:
I had over fifty meetings and handed out our beautiful little marketing brochure (a catalog of our six films with lots of infos and a DVD of all the trailers). The response was terrific, and at least half promised to review the trailers, requested screeners, and ??get?? back to us within two weeks following the market. Now I have to follow up with everyone, and we'll see how we did. We also gave out a development package for four new films to about twenty people, and we're really excited to see what happens with that. The development package consisted of a DVD demoreel for our director and a synopsis of each film. Several people have already requested to see the scripts. It was an amazing experience and the best way to understand how the market works. We learned so much.

Some Dos and Don'ts When Attending a Film Market

DO: Make appointments to meet with sales agencies in advance for the second half of the market.

DON'T: Just walk up to their booth or suite during the first few days of the market and start pitching them your movie. Remember, they're there to sell, and that is their first priority.

DO: Come to the market prepared with one-sheets/flyers of your film and a copy of your trailer.

DON'T: Be surprised if whoever it is that you're meeting requests that you send those materials to them *after* the market, when they have more time to look the materials over.

DO: Make sure to get your hands on a buyers list for the market, so you can target distributors directly afterward.

DON'T: Corner distributors in the corridors between meetings. It's their worst pet peeve ever!

Should I Have a Distributor Screening for My Film?

This is a very common question I am asked, and I understand that it makes sense for you to want to screen your newly finished masterpiece for distributors. You want them to see it on the big screen—and not with all the hurriedness of a film festival. You want distributors to view your picture the way it was meant to be viewed.

But how do distributors feel about going to screenings? Quite honestly, they would rather watch your movie from the comfort of their desks. After being in the office all day screening picture after picture, the *last* thing an acquisitions executive wants to do after work is go to a distributor screening of someone's film.

Now there are exceptions to this, of course, and I have heard of filmmakers having a couple of distributors show up for their screenings, but I wouldn't recommend allocating resources to one. Your money can be spent so much more productively elsewhere, because whether or not anyone shows up for your screening, you'll still be stuck paying for the theater and the invitations/mailout.

One exception that is quite common is when an agent holds a screening for distributors. When I worked at William Morris, we used to screen newly completed movies for U.S. distributors prior to premiering the movies at a film festival. When a picture is represented by William Morris, distributors clamor to attend the screening. There are always bidding wars right there in the screening room. This is how so many films already have U.S. distribution deals in place at festivals such as Sundance, Cannes, and Toronto.

Interview with Linda Nelson, independent filmmaker

Are you currently working with a foreign-sales agent for your film *Shifted*? Why or why not?

Currently, our film Shifted *is still playing at film festivals, so I have not actively pursued a foreign-sales agent yet. We will be screening in five more cities this fall, and have recently been invited to screen at a festival in March of 2007. I want to wait until after AFM in November to start actively approaching foreign-sales agents, so that I can collect as many good reviews and press as possible. We have sent screeners to four foreign distributors that requested to see the film after we we wrote to them, but we have not received any responses yet. We did a lot of research to find the contact information so that we could contact distributors directly, but I'm not sure we will want to take the time it will take to develop the relationships required to self-distribute to foreign markets. We are fortunate to have all the materials required for foreign distribution, so if and when we decide to use a foreign-sales agent, we will be ready. Recently, we have listed our film with three different digital-distribution platforms that are in beta on the Internet. These platforms are meant to manage a filmmaker's licensing needs, and make it easy for distributors to license film rights directly from filmmakers. We are interested to see the results of these listings. The platforms we have chosen to use are inDplay.com, and Audience at Withoutabox.com. These companies are working hard to make digital markets for independent film, and we are excited to be early users of these systems.*

What is Indie Co-Op, and what is your vision for it?

Indie Co-op is a private group on MySpace where filmmakers with completed projects can find information on self-distribution. Any member can post topics of interest to other filmmakers or ask questions about self-distribution. Originally, we formed the group as a way to disseminate distribution information, but recently several members have expressed an interest in formalizing the group as an actual company, so that films owned by members could be marketed as a catalog of films. We are finding that certain distribution outlets prefer to acquire rights to entire catalogs, rather than dealing with filmmakers one-on-one. For example, several online-distribution outlets prefer to acquire Internet downloading rights for a catalog of films. Also, as a quasi-distributor, Indie Co-op could attend markets such as AFM, sharing costs among members of the co-op. Often these markets can be very expensive. This company could also provide blocks of films to aggregators that sell film rights to large retailers like Blockbuster, Best Buy, Target, and Wal-Mart.

How has your experience at festivals been? How important do you think festivals are for distribution?

We have enjoyed the film-festival experience, especially festivals that are held in major cities where there is an opportunity for industry and press to see the films. We actually received three distribution offers prior to any festival exposure, but did not conclude any contracts. Since our film was done under a SAG agreement, it was important for us to try and negotiate a contract that included some type of advance so that the actors could get paid. So far, we have not been offered a contract with an advance. I think that festivals are very important to filmmakers for a lot of reasons. Festivals in major cities like Los Angeles are most likely to attract industry and press screenings. If your film is accepted in one of the top festivals like Sundance, Toronto, Tribeca, or Cannes, you can count on some industry exposure. If you are only able to get into smaller festivals, at least you can acquire some good quotes and reviews in local press. So far, we have gotten three great reviews that we are proud of. A collection of reviews and quotes can enhance your chance of finding distribution, and even if you are self-distributing, it helps to be able to put these reviews with your film listing. For example, we got a great review from Film Threat, which is a very respected independent-film web site. We also got a good review from Todd Schwartz, a CBS arts-and-entertainment film critic who saw our film at Dances With Films. These reviews are posted on our Amazon.com and e-commerce pages, where we are currently selling our DVD.

What have you been doing in terms of self-distribution, and how has it worked out for you?

As soon as our film was finished and we had spoken with a few distribution companies, we decided that we would try to distribute our DVD on the Internet by ourselves. There are many excellent web sites where you can sell your independent feature. Some are more obvious than others. We have a company web site, but rather than have to administer our own e-commerce, we link directly to several sites where you can purchase, rent, or download our film. We believe that you should take advantage of any non-exclusive arrangement you can make for Internet sales, providing you research the company and are comfortable that they will pay you on a regular basis and give you accurate reporting. We link to these sites from our own web site, www.nelsonmadisonfilms.com, and from our two MySpace accounts, www.myspace.com/michaelmadison and www.myspace.com/nelsonmadison. These web sites link to Amazon.com/CustomFlix.com, who actually manufacture and ship the DVDs. We have been pleased with the performance of these companies and receive checks regularly, along with emailed reports. We are currently looking into several new accounts for video-on-demand services. Withoutabox is about to launch a new service called Distribution Lab, which will enable filmmakers to sell DVDs directly from their site, where our film is also listed, and they will also have options for limited theatrical releases for filmmakers. As we speak, new technologies are emerging that will help to get our film out there. Just yesterday, Amazon.com announced Unbox, a new movie-download service. We hope to be one of the first truly independent films on the service.

Do you plan on recouping your investment in your film? If so, through which channels is it most likely?
Since our film is considered a no/low-budget film and was produced under a SAG experimental contract, all salaries were deferred. We were fortunate enough to have all our locations donated, and our great music contributed by incredible musicians. My partner, Michael Madison, and I wrote the film. Michael also edited the film, so we only have to recoup about $75K to break even. We believe that TV/cable sales and foreign sales will be our best chance for recoupment along with DVD sales. It's a little early to tell.

What has been the biggest disappointment in your journey to find distribution for your film? What has been the biggest highlight?
Our biggest disappointment was our inability to get our film into any major festivals. We spent a huge amount of time, money, and effort in preparing submissions to all the major festivals. In hindsight, I believe that without some type of industry connection, such as a producers rep or distribution company behind you, your chances of landing in a major festival are slim to nothing. I think that new filmmakers like us need to focus on smaller regional festivals, including at least one in Los Angeles and one in New York. This is important to get press and reviews so that you can then approach potential distributors. Self-distribution is becoming a real viable option for those filmmakers that are very proactive and interested in marketing their own films. Some filmmakers just prefer to turn their films over to someone else once they're finished, but others do have an interest in self-distribution. I am excited about the future of distribution, and am confident that we are in the middle of some very exciting changes in how independent films find their audiences. The biggest highlight for me has been the opportunity to meet so many wonderful people that genuinely care about the future of independent film. This year, I've met about twenty people that have started new companies totally dedicated to seeing that independent filmmakers have more of an opportunity to get their films seen.

Suggested Exercises for Part Five

1. Start a blog for your independent film. Upload stills, a trailer, production diaries, or whatever you have ready at the stage you are in.
2. List a film festival to which you are taking your film. Tell what your distribution strategy is for the festival.
3. Get in contact with a foreign-sales agent or producers rep and ask them about their submissions process, what kind of films they do well with, and so on. Write a paragraph on your findings and share with your classmates

— 6 —

Getting a Distribution Deal

The U.S. Distribution Deal and What to Expect

So how do you actually go about getting a U.S. distribution deal for your film? In the previous sections, I've discussed things you can do during each stage of the production process that will give your movie infinitely better chances at getting distribution. So now that you've done all those things, how do you actually secure a U.S. deal for yourself, and what should you expect?

First of all, as I explained before, a U.S. distribution deal has become harder and harder to come by in recent years. So actually, getting a deal is quite a feat. There are a few different avenues to focus on when considering distribution in the United States. They include the following types of U.S. distribution:

- Theatrical
- DVD
- Broadcast

Sometimes when you get a U.S. distribution deal, you sell all of these rights at once (all-rights deal), and sometimes you sell each rights group separately. There are advantages and disadvantages to both.

The advantage of selling all three of these rights groups at once to a single distributor is that, hopefully, you will see a bigger up-front payment as an advance. For example, say your picture wins an award at the Sundance Film Festival. If that is the case, you will most likely be approached by distributors who want to sign an all-rights deal with you. Realistically, the only companies that would be offering this type of deal to you are the mini-majors (the independent arms of the major studios)—they are the ones with the deep pockets. The mini-majors include Sony Pictures Classics, Warner Independent Pictures, Paramount Classics, Focus Features, Fox Searchlight, ThinkFilm, Lions Gate Entertainment, and Samuel Goldwyn Films.

The disadvantage to selling all your rights to one distributor is that whatever payment you get from that one distributor—that's it. You do not have the opportunity to go out and get additional sales on your film to make any additional money. So if the advance offered isn't enough to pay your investors back, tough luck.

During negotiations with a U.S. distributor, you should always at least *try* to carve out U.S. broadcast rights for yourself. Most likely, the big companies will not let you do this. However, if you are able to carve out those rights for yourself, you will have the opportunity to sell them directly to a broadcaster. That way, all that money will go into your pocket instead of the distributor's.

Keep in mind, though, that the reason U.S. distributors are able to pay you a high advance for your film is because they calculate they will recoup that in ancillary sales: DVD, broadcast, and foreign.

One thing to look out for when you are selling U.S. distribution rights is that many *sales agencies* (not distributors) will offer you a distribution deal for little or no advance up front. This is a very common scenario for independent films because, as you can imagine, the Sundance example I outlined above is for only a small handful of people each year. In fact, unless you get into Sundance or one of the other Tier 1 festivals, you have very little chances of getting an all-rights distribution deal with one of the mini-majors, along with the accompanying big payout.

My advice to you is this: if you get offered a distribution deal by a sales agency, look very carefully at who they are and the types of films they sell. First of all, know that they are not offering you a "distribution" deal. They are offering to take all your rights to your movie and sell off those rights to various distributors. So don't get confused by the terminology! I hear so many filmmakers saying they have been offered distribution deals—but in reality, it's just an offer from a sales agency that is going to turn around and sell your film to distributors.

Bottom line is that if you are going to sign with a sales agency for distribution, do *not* do an all-rights deal if you can help it. I would recommend signing away only the foreign rights to the sales agency, and keeping the U.S. rights for yourself. The reason is because you can always approach U.S. DVD companies and broadcasters directly; you do not necessarily need the services of a sales agency for that. However, you may want the agency's expertise with selling the foreign-distribution rights.

It is also becoming more and more common for U.S. DVD distributors to ask for foreign rights when they acquire the U.S. DVD rights to a picture. In order to recoup their advance and add to their bottom line, they have developed distribution partnerships in foreign territories, so they try and make a few foreign sales here and there to recoup their investment. So be on the lookout for this, and decide whether the advance the DVD company is offering you is worth giving up foreign rights.

How to Approach U.S. Distributors Yourself

As I said, getting a U.S. distribution deal is quite a feat. Many filmmakers ask me if they should go ahead and start submitting to U.S. distributors themselves once they have a completed project. My answer is always *not yet*.

What I recommend doing with U.S. distributors is first waiting to see if you get accepted to any of the Tier 1 film festivals. This is because if you end up premiering your film at one of those, you will have much more leverage with distributors than if you were to go to them *before* that festival.

So Plan A is to wait and see if you get into a Tier 1ne festival. However, if you are not applying to any Tier 1 festivals, or you do not get accepted to any, then go to Plan B. This means submiting to U.S. distributors yourself. Now, that doesn't mean that you should start submitting in a haphazard fashion. Rather, it means starting at the *top* and working your way down.

A good way to go about this is to research appropriate distributors for your movie, starting with the mini-majors on down to straight-to-DVD companies and cable broadcasters. Be sure to start with the bigger companies first. They are more likely than the smaller companies to want to acquire all rights for your film. If you've already sold off DVD rights to a straight-to-video company, then you will no doubt lose out on this much bigger deal.

If one of the bigger distribution companies decides to acquire your picture and take all rights, then great! If not, as you work your way down the target list you've created, just make sure that you separate out DVD companies from broadcasters, and so on.

Here is a step-by-step list of what to do should you want to approach U.S. distributors yourself:

1. Take an honest look at your movie and decide for which distributor you think it's a fit. Study distributors' web sites as well as their past and present slates. Do they distribute only movies with big cast, for example? Do they specialize in foreign films? Is everything they distribute from a star director? If your film doesn't fit into what their model is, then don't waste your time or theirs.

2. Research distributors that have had success with your type of picture. At this point, you're probably looking at straight-to-DVD distribution, so head back to the video store and see what companies put out your type of product. Make a list of these companies, then go home and investigate their web sites. You'll be able to contact an acquisitions executive from there. Prepare an email to them with a link to your web site, trailer, and synopsis. That way, they can decide if they would like to consider

your film for distribution. Once you've sent the email, wait a week. If you haven't heard anything back from them by then, it's O.K. to follow up with a phone call.

3. Research U.S. broadcasters that have had success with your type of movie. Flip through the cable channels and check out who broadcasts independent films these days. Again, go to their web sites and look for submissions guidelines. Send them an email with a link to your web site and trailer. If they get back to you and request it, send them a full screener copy of your movie. I've heard broadcast executives say that they wish more film-makers would contact them directly—so you can definitely do it yourself!

Filmmaker Case Study: David Basulto, in His Own Words

When I decided to direct my first film, I knew that the safest bet was to make a horror film. Coming from the $3–5 million–dollar budgets I had produced to a meager $30 K, I was left with many challenges. My biggest concern was making back the money I was investing.

Although I had many contacts in the distribution world from my previous films, this was an entirely new world I was entering, the micro-budget world. The good news was, there are so many new avenues of distribution. From online downloads to DVD, I felt confident I could find a home.

The bad news was, I didn't know who to turn to, as my distribution friends were late returning email and calls when they found out my new film was made for such a tiny budget. "Where was the money to be made in that?" they would say.

So I started a quest that would take me the better part of a year, taking meetings with prospective sales agents and distributors. I am lucky that I know the game a bit as far as deals and percentages. I can see how the uninformed can be taken for a nice ride, never seeing a dime from their hard work.

I ended up contacting buyers from international sales companies and pointing them to my web site to view a trailer. I was able to sell three territories this way. Lots of work, but at least I made 50 percent of my cash back! The beauty of this age we are in is, we can do research online for just about anything now. I decided to start pursuing domestic distribution.

After a long, arduous search, with many deals that would include no up-front moneys, I was very fortunate to meet Doug Schwab from Maverick Entertainment. Maverick specializes in smaller films straight to the DVD markets. After a week of negotiating, we made a deal that included a payment schedule. The first payment was made exactly on my delivering the elements of the film. I was impressed with the professionalism. And I made back my film's investment!

All in all, the experience was a bit stressful at times, but I gained a world of knowledge and am ready to tackle it again! My film Death Clique *is currently in Blockbuster, Netflix, and Amazon.*

Foreign Distribution and What to Expect

So now that you know how to go about getting a U.S. distribution deal for your film, how about getting foreign distribution? Unfortunately, foreign-distribution deals don't bring in the money they once did, but the good news is that there are still several types of foreign-distribution deals to be made.

I'll start by saying that if you're lucky enough to get an all-rights deal from a U.S. distributor (for example, one of the mini-majors), you won't have to worry about getting foreign distribution for your film. It will be distributed in foreign territories through the various partnerships that exist between U.S. mini-majors and foreign theatrical and DVD distributors and foreign broadcasters. How does this work? Because most of the mini-majors fall under the big umbrella of a studio (for example, Focus Features is part of Universal Studios, and Warner Independent Pictures is part of Warner Bros.), they automatically get to take advantage of the output deals that exist with foreign-distribution channels, as well as international operations such as local offices.

For the mini-majors that do not fall under an umbrella of a studio (ThinkFilm, Lions Gate Entertainment, and others), the situation is a little different. Fortunately, by virtue of having U.S. theatrical distribution through one of these high-level companies, you will have a much easier time finding foreign distribution, because these nonstudio mini-majors are so well respected. For example, if you have U.S. theatrical distribution for your picture through Think-Film, you will most likely be picked up by one of the top foreign-sales agencies, who will then secure foreign-distribution deals for your movie.

If you do *not* have U.S. theatrical distribution for your film, then there are still a few avenues you can take to sell your project to foreign territories:

- Through a U.S. DVD distributor
- Through a U.S. broadcaster
- Through a foreign-sales agency
- Do-it-yourself

Through a U.S. DVD Distributor

Certain U.S. DVD distributors will ask for worldwide rights when acquiring your film. The reason is because several of these companies have developed partnerships in foreign territories and have created their own mini-output deals. So, for example, say you get offered a U.S. DVD deal by XYZ distributor, and they request worldwide rights. They will then go and offer your picture to their foreign partners, and give you a percentage of whatever advance has been agreed upon. Obviously, the benefit of this arrangement to the U.S. distributor is that any foreign sales they make on your movie will help their own bottom line. In the past, this wasn't a very common solution—most U.S. DVD companies didn't want to be bothered with the intricate business of foreign sales. But once they discovered that they could simply establish relationships with a few reliable partners in each territory (similar to the studio model), it became more appealing to them.

The benefit to you, of course, is that you have an automatic foreign-sales agent working for you to sell worldwide DVD rights to your film. So you do not have to worry about trying to sell these rights yourself, or hiring a sales rep to do it for you. It's all part of your U.S. deal. Before you sign over the worldwide DVD rights to your U.S. distributor, however, the one thing you want to make sure about is what their results have been in making foreign deals on other films in their catalog. Before you sign a deal with them, ask for filmmaker references so you can contact some people that they work with to see what their experience has been, to make sure they got accounted to and paid properly for any foreign sales that were made, and so forth. You can also ask the U.S. DVD company what their results have been, and what they project your picture can do in foreign sales, and then decide if you want to tie up all your rights with them.

Through a U.S. Broadcaster

There are also certain U.S. broadcasters who will ask for worldwide rights when acquiring your property. For example, Discovery Channel, Lifetime, Hallmark Channel, History Channel, and many other networks all broadcast on cable systems throughout the world. Therefore, if Lifetime acquires your film for U.S. broadcast, they will most likely ask for worldwide broadcast rights as well. What's different here from the DVD scenario is that they will not be selling your film to third-party broadcasters, but rather, keeping it for their own network in the different foreign territories. So you won't be getting any percentages of foreign sales as in the DVD example. Therefore, you want to make sure that you are fairly compensated for signing away worldwide foreign-broadcast rights to your film.

If you think you can get more money by selling the international broadcast rights separately or on your own, then limit your deal with the U.S. broadcaster to U.S. rights alone. Keep in mind, however, that foreign-broadcast rights are much tougher to secure than foreign-DVD rights, so don't shoot yourself in the foot by thinking you can do it all yourself. To decide if you would even have a chance, make sure you do adequate research into some foreign broadcasters and what types of independent films they are programming.

Through a Foreign-Sales Agency

I've already described what a foreign-sales agent is and how to go about getting one. Working with a foreign-sales agent can be very effective in getting international distribution for your movie. The main reason is because that is what they are dedicated to. Their whole reason for being is finding international distribution deals for independent films.

One benefit of working with a foreign-sales agent is that they will bear the cost of taking your picture to all the international film markets, and therefore exposing your work to a very large contingent of buyers from all over the world. Going to the film markets is no cheap expense, and is something you'd be hard-pressed to do on your own. For this reason alone, there is a huge value in working with a foreign-sales agent.

One downside to working with such an agent is that their high costs of doing business get passed on to you in the form of high commissions per sale and recoupable expenses allowed. Therefore, at the end of the day, you may not actually see much money from the foreign-distribution deals—because the first $30K to $50K in sales will go toward covering the agency's marketing and other hard costs. This is frustrating for many filmmakers (understandably so). Because the acquisitions prices in the international marketplace are so low to begin with, working with a foreign-sales agent almost always means the filmmaker will never see a cent.

Do-It-Yourself

If the thought of working with a foreign-sales agent doesn't appeal to you, then you can always go the do-it-yourself route. However, I must warn you that the do-it-yourself route to foreign distribution is not only more difficult than that in the United States, but much more expensive. Be prepared for shipping costs, high phone bills, travel expenses, and film-market expenses.

If you decide to go for it anyway, then the first question is: Who *are* the foreign DVD companies and broadcasters that buy independent films? You can buy lists on the Internet, but are they current and correct? Honestly, the best advice I have here is to see if you can get some word-of-mouth recommendations from other film-makers who have gotten foreign distribution. Then start contacting these companies directly. Internet message boards are a great source of word-of-mouth recommendations for foreign buyers.

The best approach I have found for filmmakers to contact foreign distributors directly is first via email (send an introductory email with a link to your web site and trailer), and then follow up with a phone call. If the distributor requests a screening copy of your film, be sure to send it via FedEx, UPS, or DHL so that you can get a tracking number. It is customary to follow up with an email and phone call to make sure your package was received.

Another way to track down foreign buyers is to attend the international film markets. Filmmakers are now creating co-ops and pooling their funds together to get a booth in the actual market. This can be an affordable option if you can get five to ten filmmakers together. Once you are registered as a seller at a film market, you will be given access to the entire list of buyers. This list is golden—it will not only serve you for the particular market you are attending, but for long after the market is over. Once you have access to the buyers list prior to a market, it is customary to send out emails requesting meetings with buyers. Of course, you will need to come up with a listing of all the films you're selling at the market, complete with JPEG images of the cover art. You can email this list, and direct buyers to your web site(s), where they can view trailers. The goal is to set up as many appointments as possible for the market. Once you are there, you should hire someone to be in the booth with you. This should be somone who has experience selling at a market. It will be well worth the money—their services will end up paying for themselves.

Interview with Hamish McAlpine of Tartan Films (U.K.) (*Black Book, Brothers of the Head*)

For Tartan, is it vital for a filmmaker to have a U.S. theatrical release if they want to have a U.K. theatrical release for their film?
No, it is not vital for Tartan to have a film be released theatrically in the

U.S. primarily because U.S. audiences often have different tastes to U.K. audiences. A U.S. theatrical release (provided it is a success) will. However, give U.K. distributors more confidence in booking a film.

What about straight-to-video releases? Do you ever do straight-to-video releases with your acquisitions?
It is primarily only some Asia Extreme titles that go direct-to-video. We do, of course, release many classic films (Bergman, Eisenstein, Pasolini, Ozu, etc,).

As one of the biggest distributors in the United Kingdom, does Tartan actually release non-British films? And do you place emphasis on whether or not a potential acquisition was in any specific festivals?
Virtually all the films we release in the U.K. are non-British films. An official film-festival entry (preferably in competition and at one of the top five festivals) is what we prefer.

Do you accept submissions directly from filmmakers? Where do you acquire most of your films—at festivals and markets?
We only accept submissions directly from filmmakers if they are personally known to us. Otherwise we would be swamped, and our acquisitions department would go into meltdown. We acquire most of our films from sales agents or from American agencies. Most of our acquisitions occur at festivals or markets.

How do you feel about working with sales agents for your acquisitions? Do you prefer that to dealing directly with filmmakers?
We prefer to work directly with sales agents rather than filmmakers because 99 percent of filmmakers are not set up to make full delivery, and also never seem to have the time available when problems occur. We do, of course, love working directly with filmmakers in terms of marketing their films, but materials invariably put a spoke in relationships.

Any suggestions for filmmakers who do not have a sales agent for their films and wish to get U.K. distribution?
If they do not have a sales agent for their films, and their films are not adequately represented at film festivals, then the best thing to do is to organize a drinks reception followed by a film screening in one of London's screening hotels (Charlotte Street Hotel, Covent Garden Hotel, etc.) for all the U.K. distributors.

Does Tartan ever prebuy films? If so, what are the requirements?
Yes, Tartan does prebuy films. Normally, they are films made by directors with whom Tartan has a previous relationship (Claire Denis, Michael Haneke, John Hillcoat, etc,). Sometimes we prebuy films from producers who have an existing track record with Tartan.

Expenses Required to Market and Distribute a Film

Whether you sign directly with a distributor, go through a foreign-sales agency, or self-distribute, you should be familiar with the expenses required to market and distribute a picture. This is especially true because you will be charged these expenses before you are allowed to share in the profits.

As you can imagine, it is very expensive to market and distribute an independent film. That is why when you sign a deal with a distributor, they will require that they are allowed to recoup anywhere from $10K to $25K (in some cases more) before they begin sharing profits with you. Because they are investing this much in marketing and distributing your movie, it is only fair that they get their investment back through sales.

When you are signed on with a U.S. distributor or foreign-sales agency, you will be accounted to every quarter, biyearly, or yearly in a producers report. The producers report will outline the expenses incurred for the period in question, and you will be able to see how close the distributor is to recouping the contractual marketing expenses. Once the distributor recoups the agreed amount of expenses, you will start receiving checks with your producers report for your portion of the profit share.

Normally, you can expect to receive a producers report or accounting statement thirty to forty-five days *after* the quarter, or half, or year has ended. So if you are due quarterly accounting reports, and the first quarter ends on September 30, then you should get your accounting report around October 30 or November 15.

Here's what a typical expense report might look like if you are doing a theatrical release for your film:

April 30, 2006
Stacey Parks
P.O. Box 72A
Los Angeles, CA 90261
Type: Feature Film
Territory: Worldwide
Per distribution agreement dated November 24, 2003
Term ends: November 24, 2010
For the period ended September 30, 2006
GROSS RECEIPTS
   International receipts $10,000
   Domestic receipts $20,000
Total Gross Receipts $30,000
DISTRIBUTION FEES AND MARKETING EXPENSES
   Distribution fee   25% = $7,500
   Market fee expense $10,000
   Promotional expenses $15,000
   Delivery expenses $5,000
Total Distribution fees and expenses $37,500

A few things to note from this report:

- This is a sample report from a foreign-sales agent to a filmmaker.
- Note that the expenses for this period were higher than the revenue, meaning that the filmmaker doesn't receive any of the revenue.
- There is a film market somewhere in the world practically every quarter, so you can expect to see these charges on every report.
- Most importantly, you will not be paid any profits until your accumulated sales revenue surpasses the expenses cap agreed to in the contract. So make sure the cap you agree to is as low as possible!

Filmmaker Case Study: Robert Brinkmann, in His Own Words

Robert Brinkmann talks about finding distribution for his independent film *Stephen Tobolowsky's Birthday Party*.

I really had no idea how much work it would be to do this release our-selves. Had I known then what I know now, we might have taken one of those offers that looked so bad at the time. We have spent a lot of money and an enormous amount of time getting the DVD out and promoting sales. Though we have had enormous success with press attention—just go to our web site (www.stbpmovie.com) or Google the name of the film to check it out.

I doubt anyone could have done better in terms of free publicity: from multiple appearances on CNN to the front page of the L.A. Times *Sunday Calendar section, from radio appearances all over the country to wonder-fully supportive reviews (including two in* Variety*!), we have had more press than any microbudgeted film can possibly hope for. Despite all this press, however, I have learned that it is necessary to be readily available to the customer. Even with the readily accessible Internet, there is a fairly high threshold to get somebody to buy your DVD.*

Here is something to consider when thinking about self-distribution: all of this attention does not give us the same amount of sales as the com-plete turkey of a movie Warner Bros. releases straight-to-DVD. Any studio, through their retail partnerships, ships more units on something that is completely unwatchable than we can sell on the Internet—just because they have a certain amount of sales built in through retailers who will order a package of their releases. It is hard to compete with these guys, and not as easy to sell over the Internet as you might think.

Of course, you will sell to people who are interested in what you are doing or who know you or your principals. What's harder is to get others, who may be curious or have heard about your project, to get on the com-puter, pull out their wallet, and place an order. Anytime we slow down with our promotion, we notice a drop in sales. That's why we decided to go on a tour of the Apple stores and give a presentation on the making of our film (don't worry, Stephen will be there and entertain the audience, so it won't be technical or boring—the calendar of appearances is on our site) to keep awareness up. We started our promotion during the festival run of our film, and redoubled our efforts with our self-release on May 30 of this year. I have run into so many people who have heard about Stephen Tobolowsky's Birthday Party *and are curious about it (and have no idea I was involved, so it is not through me) but have not ordered it. Think about that: they know of the film and want to see it—but they don't buy it! I am convinced that, if they saw it in front of them in a store, we would have gotten a sale.*

For this reason, we are backtracking a bit and talking to distributors and sales agents about helping us get the film into stores. I think, after the experience so far, that seeing the product and being able to hold it in your hands makes a difference to a lot of potential buyers. Though the profit margin will be much lower (we make three times as much on a DVD sold on our web site as on one sold through a distributor), the numbers more than make up for the discrepancy. And even though we have been able to get into some stores, it is way too involved to try and get into as many as is necessary.

We have one great advantage—we don't have to sell. We have a viable commercial product, and can wait if necessary to find a deal we like. Usually, making a film is so expensive that it is hard for producers to hold out. Of course, distributors know this, and can use the financial pressure to their advantage. HDNet—one of the natural outlets for films produced on HD, and a good match for us—had enough interest from their viewers to approach us about distribution, but their offer was so low that we would have broken even at best. Since we could afford to wait, we turned them down. Any producer who mortgaged their house would have had to take their offer not to lose it.

As far as the effect of marketing is concerned, it has been very hard to see a direct correlation. When Stephen flew to Chicago to spend an hour on WGN's Nick at Night, we didn't have any sales in Chicago that weekend, but an uptick in the South. We have had a fair amount of sales in Chicago, though, so his three appearances on the show (we were extremely lucky that Nick is a fan of Stephen's) clearly had an effect. Stephen's philosophy is that you just have to keep plugging, and that no marketing effort is a waste—it will all add up and eventually lead to critical mass, and then the whole thing takes off. Since we can't spend any money on this effort, we just do everything we can, and consider nothing a waste or a dead end.

The best advice I can give any filmmaker is to make sure that you have a unique angle to sell your product (in our case, it's that guy!), and a performer with a vested interest in the outcome of the release, so that the support to publicize the film is built in. Even then, think long and hard about whether self-distribution is the way to go.

My hope for the future is that the delivery of films will change along the same lines as music distribution. Once Apple sells everyone's movies through the iTunes Store, independents will have an easier time reaching the consumer. (I know there are other services, but I'm biased toward Apple, and think they will be more successful at it.) It will be a road around the entrenched interests, who protect their turf and may not always be honest, and directly to the end user.

Suggested Exercises for Part Six

1. Contact five U.S. and five foreign distributors and ask if you can submit your film. What are their requirements for submission?
2. Pretend your instructor or partner is a U.S. distributor. Pitch him or her your movie and why he or she should distribute it. Who is your market? Hint: now's a great time to showcase your market research. Post your pitch on the discussion board.

— 7 —

After the Distribution Deal

Congratulations! You got distribution for your film. Now what? What can you expect to happen?

So many filmmakers think that once they get a distribution deal for their movie, all their hard work is over. Unfortunately, it is just not the case. Realistically, expect to continue your marketing efforts because although any distributor will create a marketing campaign of their own for your picture, no one can market it as well as you can. And distributors have more than just your movie to contend with in their catalogs, so anything extra you can do to help drive sales will ultimately help your own bottom line.

And remember, the squeaky wheel gets the oil. Feel free to call or email your distributor with any suggestions you have for creative marketing or promotions. Also, don't be afraid to ask for your producers report or accounting statement whenever it's due. Take an active interest in the success of your film, and it will be successful.

If the distributor needs more artwork or slides from you, or a clean master, go and get it done right away. The longer you take to turn in all your deliverables, the longer your picture will sit there without getting any sales push. Work with your distributor as if you were partners, and pay attention to even the smallest of details, so that your film gets the chance in the marketplace that it deserves.

When Will I Get Paid?: Distribution Cash Flow

Another aspect of distribution deals that you want to be clear on is how distribution cash flow works. Some filmmakers assume that the moment their distribution deal closes, a check will come in the mail. Not the case at all. And the worst thing you can do is depend on your movie's sales revenue for paying the rent or time-sensitive bills. The truth is, it can take a while before money starts actually hitting your account.

Another important reason for understanding distribution cash flow is so you can give realistic timelines to your investors on when they will start seeing repayment of their investment. The fact that it's going to take a while is O.K., but you need to be up front with people so they know what they're in for *before* they invest in your film.

Also, it helps you to know when money is going to start rolling in so you can start planning for your next project. As a general guideline, here is what you can expect in terms of distribution cash flow:

All-Rights Deal

If you are lucky enough to get an all-rights deal from one of the mini-majors, then your nice big advance (hopefully!) will probably be processed within thirty days after signature of the hard-copy agreements, verified QC of your master, and all the delivery items on their list. I have seen it take three to four months or more to get signed hard copies of contracts in place after making a deal, so plan on three to six months after agreeing to the deal before you see your first check. Usually, the first check will be for a percentage of the total advance amount, with the balance remaining paid out over installments.

U.S. DVD Deal

With a U.S. DVD deal, the norm for cash flow is 50 percent of the agreed-upon advance on signature of contracts, and the remaining

50 percent payment on full delivery of all materials and verified QC of your master. Sometimes, DVD companies will want to pay you the second 50 percent payment several months later—say, on the release date of the film. I recommend negotiating against this option; otherwise you'll be stuck waiting for six months to a year to see your second payment.

Also, with a U.S. DVD deal, you will receive royalty payments. I recommend negotiating for quarterly statements and payments so that you recoup your money more quickly. Otherwise they may try to negotiate your getting yearly or twice-yearly accounting.

U.S. Broadcast Deal

With a U.S. broadcast deal, typically you will get paid 50 percent upon signature of contracts and verified QC of master, and the other 50 percent on the first date of airing. The catch here is that oftentimes the airdate will be six to eight months later—meaning you won't see that second payment for quite some time. You can try to negotiate that they move up the airdate, or that you get paid 100 percent upon signature of contracts and QC, but that is unlikely to happen.

One other thing to be aware of with a broadcast deal in particular is that it takes a *long* time to get hard copies of contracts generated. Count on between two and three months, maybe even more. So plan on waiting this amount of time before receiving your first payment from broadcasters.

Foreign-Distribution Deals

With foreign-distribution deals, the cash-flow situation can be surprisingly promising if you are selling to reputable DVD companies and broadcasters. I know that's a big *if* in the foreign marketplace, but you can usually use your common sense to discern which distribution companies are reputable and which are not.

For example, most foreign DVD companies will offer you 50 percent payment upon signature of contracts, and *you* get to draft the contracts (using the standard AFMA/IFTA template). That means, you don't have to wait for anyone else's business department to generate contracts; rather, you have control over how quickly they get drafted, signed, and sent over to the buyer for countersignature.

I have also seen many foreign distributors offer 100 percent payment up front. Then you know they're a serious buyer! Obviously, the key is to negotiate as much as you can up front—and if you get only 50 percent (which is great), negotiate for the second 50 percent payment upon delivery of materials and verified QC of your master.

A lot of foreign buyers will try and spread out payments over four equal installments, but do not fall for this. It might sound tempting as you get swept up in the excitement of having a distributor interested in your film, but trust me, I've had nothing but bad experiences with foreign buyers and payment plans. Also remember that with foreign distribution, you won't be counting on royalty payments, so you want to try and negotiate as much up front as possible.

One last thing to keep in mind is that it's not as easy to track down or stay on top of foreign distributors as it is with ones in your own country. When a payment goes missing, there's not much you can do as recourse. Also, your payments will be coming via foreign money wire, so keep that in mind as well. From the time the buyer says they have wired the money, it could take up to one week or longer just to reach your account, especially with the level of security over bank wires these days.

Interview with Stephen Winter, producer of the indie success *Tarnation*

Everybody knows *Tarnation* as the film that was made for $215, was cut on iMovie, and got a big distribution deal. How did distribution happen for this film?
I remember at Sundance, we would have these amazing screenings with people weeping for joy at Tarnation, *pronouncing Jonathan a genius, everything, the whole cake and cream. Then people would come up to me,*

the producer, with this woeful "Oh dear . . ." look on their face. After wiping tears from their eyes and congratulating me up the wazoo, they'd pull me to a private corner and explain exactly why Tarnation will never, ever be screened again. The music clearances and TV/film licensing, so integral to the film's aesthetics, will be far too complicated and expensive for a distributor to take on. The subject matter is too intense. It doesn't fit into a genre box, being both a documentary and experimental. It's too this, not enough that; there's never been anything like it before; and on and on. Just the most depressing conversations I have ever had in my life. Especially considering the effort and blood it took for Jonathan, I, and the Tarnation team, which at that time was quite small, just to get the movie off of Jonathan's computer in Queens, onto an Avid in Manhattan, and pare it down from two rough-hewed hours to ninety complete minutes.

I shielded Jonathan from all the nay-saying, of course, and let him know we didn't need to leave Sundance with a deal to consider ourselves a success. And of course, all the nay-saying got me down. But I knew it would be an uphill battle for Tarnation *to grab the prize of distribution when I first saw it, as a two–and-a-half-hour cut, on VHS, that Jonathan gave me in August of 2003. And now, a scant five months later, we had made Sundance! An incredible amount of work happened in a very short time. The film had taken a life of its own; it was out of the chute and breathing in the crisp, cold Sundance air. The film would grow, I knew it would. All we needed was more time and faith.*

What was your festival strategy?

We went the uncharted route. This film had a birth unlike any other I could think of in the sense it came directly from the street—not the film-school system or Indiewood, or from moneyed backers or foreign territory. It came from the heartland and from Jonathan's heart. Our big break at Sundance came when we were invited to Cannes. That was our second lifeline, but also a real long shot. Unlike Sundance, there is no "Slam-Cannes." Either you have the money to pay for hotels, publicists, lobster dinners, publicity materials, manpower, French cell phones, trade ads, and, most important, a perfectly subtitled 35mm print, or you ain't going to Cannes! We presented at Sundance with a digital cut, 'cause they do that there. Cannes is different. So with Gus Van Sant, John Cameron Mitchell, Jonathan, about a dozen angels, and myself, we hit the streets looking for funds. And yes, it was all no, no, no—endlessly no—until Ryan Werner, Vanessa Arteaga, and Marie Therese Guirgis, the visionary team at Wellspring 2004, saw it and moved their corporate heaven and earth to acquire us. Then it was a race to get that print ready and get the Cannes ducks in a row. Then we went to Cannes, and then the rest was, well, easier than before. The festivals we went to after Cannes included New York, Chicago, Los Angeles Independent, London, and Toronto.

When did you come on board? When did John Cameron Mitchell and Gus Van Sant come board?
John Cameron Mitchell and I are best friends. In spring of 2003, Jonathan auditioned for John's new film Shortbus *and showed him part of* Tarnation. *John adored Jonathan and encouraged him to call me, saying his friend Stephen was a filmmaker too. He didn't say I should come on board—and at that point, Jonathan wasn't looking for anyone to come aboard anything. John just thought Jonathan and I would get along and we ought to meet. And remember, Jonathan didn't make* Tarnation *with the aim of doing anything more than showing it to a few friends. Or he just wanted it out there, but didn't know what exactly "out there" meant. When I saw the film, I had a good idea where it might end up somewhere great, and no matter what, I would put all my muscle behind getting it to that place. I absolutely loved the film, and knew Jonathan and I would work together splendidly. By trade, I was an indie filmmaker, so I brought to it that eye, and I had long made a living producing TV like Lifetime, VH1, etc., so I had those nuts-and-bolts skills too. Later, JCM brought the film to Gus in Portland, and he fell in love with it too, becoming our patron saint. It was the confluence of our collective energies that propelled Jonathan and* Tarnation *over the mountaintop.*

Did having Gus Van Sant's and John Cameron Mitchell's names on the project influence distribution?
Ya gotta have some kind of name recognition at Sundance to split through all the maze of films there! Remember, we were at Sundance in 2004, the year of Saw, Garden State, Primer, *and* Napolean Dynamite. *Only the former two of those films had names, but the latter had comedy and sci-fi—proven genres to help propel them. We had a new genre, at that time unnamed, since then dubbed by the* New York Times *as "narci-cinema." We had so-called challenging subject matter. And to top it off, we were a late entry, so we were out of the competition and ineligible for the documentary prize. We were in the Frontiers section. And keep in mind, even though we went in with John and Gus's names attached, we didn't leave with distribution. That happened after months more work of hammering and hustling the streets for coin. The names helped get* Tarnation *in the door, but it was the quality of filmmaking that kept us in the room.*

What made *Tarnation* attractive to distributors both domestically and internationally?

You need to get one heavy hitter to say yes, and say they want something—then everyone else who has been wavering or ignoring jumps on board. What made Tarnation *attractive?* Tarnation *was new, refreshing, exciting, emotionally invigorating, visually and aurally dazzling, experimental in nature but adhering strictly to narrative conventions. Artistically, it's airtight! A great film with a great behind-the-scenes story and a likable, talented, gregarious, and aggressive director/producer team. It's the one-of-a-kind film out of nowhere that I believe most people go into the business of film in order to find and help get behind. In the press, Jonathan got compared to the debuts of everyone from Todd Haynes to John Cassavetes, and I think that is correct.* Tarnation *was as vitalizing to film in 2004 as* Shadows *and* Superstar *were. And we created a business model that made sense. We would bring in the final product to theaters for under $500 K, just like folks used to do in indie film in the nineties and eighties, and we did it. We delivered. And finally, people leave the theater after* Tarnation *astonished. That doesn't happen every day.*

Which foreign territories has the movie sold in? How has it performed outside the United States?

We sold about twenty territories at last count, and the film draws in good numbers everywhere it goes. France and England were exceptional.

If you had to do it all over again, would you do anything different?

Oh honey, of course! But at the same time, I wouldn't change a thing. It's a really incredible thing to go charging off into the face of the unknown. I could have led myself, Jonathan, and his entire family into financial and emotional oblivion if we failed. But you know, we couldn't fail, because the film itself was too powerful. We believed in the film and fed off of its energy. Tarnation *had to be seen—we had no choice. We just went forward blind and on faith. The best way, eh?*

How has *Tarnation* changed the face of independent filmmaking?

I don't know yet. That's up to independent filmmaking to see how it will allow itself to be changed. Now that the film can be purchased on DVD, watched at home by young filmmakers, admired by seasoned ones, as it enters academia, the calendars of revival houses, written up in books and thesis projects, examined as a touchstone, reviled as a fraud, rented by kids on Netflix who live far from the cities in the middle of nowhere, used as stocking stuffers for development-studio executives . . . who knows? It hasn't changed how hard it is to get a gig in this business. Jonathan and I have been, together and as a team, working to put together new projects— and it's just as uphill a battle as it ever was. But we have Tarnation *under our belts now, and we have faith.*

Suggested Exercises for Part Seven

1. Prepare a little business plan for your film, something to present to potential investors, showcasing potential sales projections and cash-flow scenarios. Even though by this point you may have already gotten a distribution deal for your movie, prepare something for a future project now that you know what to expect.

— 8 —

Self-Distribution and Other Alternatives to Traditional Distribution

Filmmaker Case Study: Tamar Halpern, in Her Own Words

A popular term, do-it-yourself, has become a concept so suddenly well known that it need only be used in its anacronymic form. Reams of magazines devoted to D.I.Y. lifestyles and fashion, television shows which depict D.I.Y. gardening and interior design, even the use in sentences such as "We're promoting our band through D.I.Y. venues like MySpace" have elevated the concept from subculture to mainstream.

D.I.Y. also describes what those of us in the independent-film world have been doing for years. Not privy to the world of studios, production deals, or distribution offers with money up front, savvy D.I.Y. filmmakers have been scrapping and cobbling our Franken-movies together by any means possible. I am one of those filmmakers, despite being unaware there was a term for my endeavors until recently.

I could go on about the sacrifices and exploitations, the guerrilla tactics, the occasional cease-and-desist letter—but those stories have been told time and time again. What I'd like to relate instead is a story of a small success that took place at my local video store, a small success that will no doubt fuel me with the fire needed to continue on as a D.I.Y. filmmaker.

When my feature film Shelf Life *won the Grand Jury prize at its first festival (Dances With Films 2005), I was hopeful it might get some attention. My first film,* Memphis Bound and Gagged, *had won three of its first festival screenings, and nothing happened beyond that—but still, I was hopeful my second feature would create a buzz in the distribution world. Somehow it didn't. Then* Variety *published an astoundingly glowing review of* Shelf Life, *and once again I hoped that something, somehow would happen. Nada. Frustrated and baffled, I worked with a graphic designer to use some of the rave quotes from* Variety *to decorate the cover of my DVD. I sent a few to potential distributors. Again, nothing.*

I made contact with Stacey Parks, who suggested I visit my local video store, Video Journeys, and research distribution companies who were releasing independent (read: D.I.Y.) films such as my own. For some strange reason, I grabbed two copies of Shelf Life *on my way to the video store. When I arrived, I boldly plopped them down on the return desk. The clerk glanced at them and politely asked me what they were. I answered, "My film." He said, "Great," and pointed me to the area which housed the "Free Rentals—Local Filmmakers." I then did something that was really strange, even for a woman who prides herself on her tenacity. I told him my films were for sale. I suppose I was emboldened by the fact that I was a longtime customer, or maybe it was the* Variety *review, or maybe it was the fear that my second film would also fade into obscurity like my first. But whatever the reason, telling someone my films were for sale changed everything.*

The owner, citing the fact that I had been a loyal customer for many years, agreed to buy my two copies. She asked me what I wanted, and I, wholly unprepared for the conversation to even get this far, predictably had no freaking idea what to charge. She suggested a price, and I accepted. Although I won't quote the price here, I can tell you the video store made its money back almost ten fold in the first six months.

Both copies of Shelf Life *were placed in the New Release section, and each time I came in to rent a movie, the employees would look up the numbers on my film rentals and report them. I was both giddy with glee and astonishment each time I heard the numbers climbing. A couple months later, one of the supporting actors started his first semester at the University of Southern California. Another freshman came up to him and exclaimed, "I know you! You were in that movie* Shelf Life! *My family rented it, and it was hilarious!" The actor—who wasn't really an actor, but rather, a teenager who I thought would be perfect for the small role he played—was dumbfounded. Upon hearing the story, I was amazed that* Shelf Life *had found an audience that extended out of my zip code.*

For the four months that Shelf Life *sat in the New Release section, surrounded by blockbusters and newly mastered classics with huge stars and budgets, I was thrilled to know it had finally found an audience. For a while, I toyed with the idea of filling my car with* Shelf Life *DVDs and touring the country, making just enough for gas, food, and lodging, as I hawked my film to other independent video stores in true D.I.Y. fashion. Luckily, I was able to land a distribution deal instead, using my sales numbers from my local video store to create interest in the deal.*

It would have been easy to walk in my local video store that day and quietly research D.I.Y. titles, never saying a word to anyone. But if I didn't do it, who would?

Like many filmmakers, Tamar Halpern has caught on to the fact that if all else fails, there's always self-distribution. And with today's technology, self-distribution is easier than ever. Numerous tools are available to promote your film in order to attract a distributor, as well as sell your film directly to end users.

Of course, there are both upsides and downsides to self-distribution. In my opinion, the biggest upside is that any sale you make, any distribution deal you sign, you get to keep all the money for yourself. It goes directly to your bottom line—paying your investors back and adding to your profit. Conversely, the biggest downside to self-distribution that I can think of is that in exchange for not having to pay anyone a sales commission or fee or percentage of sales, you have to do all the work, which can be an enormous amount.

Don't be fooled: self-distribution takes a tremendous amount of work and patience, but it can pay off handsomely to those who are consistent with their efforts. Before I got a publisher for this book, I self-distributed it as an e-book online. And what made it a successful venture? For me, the number one thing was my consistent efforts at tirelessly marketing my product. Some weeks were good; some weeks were bad—but being absolutely consistent in my marketing efforts was, I believe, the top contributor to the book's success.

With all the self-distribution channels I talk about below, remember that because you do not have a distribution company behind you, you will have to do all the marketing, promotions, and advertising yourself—whatever it takes to drive sales of your movie. With each self-distribution method I discuss, I will talk about specific ways to market your film.

Here's another example of self-distribution that demonstrates some of the difficulties with that method:

Self-distribution is a very tiring process. The most important thing is to produce a film that some segment of the public will relate to, so that you have a market, even if it is specialized. We were lucky enough to release our feature documentary—Naked in Ashes, *about the Yogis of India*—*on the heels of a couple other films that had proven there is a marketplace for Spiritual Cinema, a term coined by Stephen Simon.* What the Bleep Do We Know!? *and* Short Cut to Nirvana *had proven to the theater exhibitors that there is an appetite for films of a spiritual nature, and that they can do business.*

Self-distribution can either be done through a reputable theater booker, as we did, or totally on your own, which takes even more elbow grease. The most important thing is to determine who is honest, and try to deal with them only. Find out the reputations of publicists, video distributors, etc., as you go through each step. The very best source of information is other filmmakers—talk to them.

If you can afford it, get a local publicist in each market—they will have the best connections locally. Market to your core audience: groups, clubs, etc. And try to generate buzz about your film in the least expensive way—through the Internet. Besides that, postcards and flyers. The most expensive thing is publicity. Even the smallest ad in a newspaper—called a topper—will cost thousands of dollars when running for a few weeks. If you get good reviews, use them as much as possible.

—Paula Fouce *(Naked in Ashes)*

On-Demand DVD Distribution

On-demand DVD distribution is one of the easiest and most profitable do-it-yourself distribution strategies. You are able to sell professional-quality DVDs without stocking your own inventory (and storing it in your spare room or garage). Instead, the on-demand

DVD companies manufacture and ship discs as customers order them.

On-demand DVD distribution is an affordable and low-risk way to make your film available to millions of customers. Furthermore, you get to keep control of your title and earn royalties from dollar one. Plus, you are free to remove your picture at any time should you land a traditional distribution deal.

Rather than wasting time managing production of your DVD and shipping the orders yourself, you're able to focus on marketing your movie. Meanwhile, the on-demand DVD companies handle the order taking, manufacturing of units, shipping, and customer support.

When you open up your film to the massive audience online, there is an opportunity for your work to be discovered and for people to buy your movie. Several filmmakers I know have landed traditional distribution deals after they have successfully built buzz by selling their projects through on-demand DVD channels.

To get started with on-demand DVD distribution, you'll need to own all the needed rights to your film, and it must meet certain content guidelines. Usually, there is a onetime setup fee of around $50, and you send the company your DVD master. If you don't have a DVD master, these companies will even digitize your film for you from a tape format. Then you set your title's suggested list price, and they will send you commission checks, normally on a monthly basis.

Unlike traditional distribution deals, with on-demand DVD companies, you maintain the rights to your work. And there is normally no commitment period or exclusive terms, so you can sell it on as many on-demand DVD sites as you wish.

The way the sales channel works is that upon sign-up, you are given your own turnkey web site, or "e-store," to sell your film. You are responsible for generating traffic to your e-store, which is where clever marketing and buzz building come in handy.

The biggest player in on-demand DVD distribution is Custom-Flix (www.customflix.com), which is actually owned by Amazon.com. When you use the CustomFlix service, you are guaranteed exposure to the tens of millions of customers who visit Amazon.

com on a daily basis. Having that kind of built-in audience makes the job of driving sales to your e-store that much easier.

Internet Distribution/Video on Demand (VOD)

In contrast to on-demand DVD distribution, where the end user receives a physical DVD disc of your movie, video-on-demand (VOD) distribution allows the end user to download your movie to their computer and watch it right then and there.

There are several companies out there offering different types of services, but in general the way it works is that you send the VOD company a DVD master of your film, they digitize it and upload it to their servers, and then customers pay a fee to download your film and watch it. The download time, of course, varies by type of VOD service and speed of a customer's Internet connection, but the idea is that instead of waiting for a DVD to be shipped, the customer has instant access to the purchased movie.

In terms of revenue, just as with on-demand DVD companies, VOD companies also send you monthly checks for your share of the revenue. For example, if the VOD company charges $9.99 for a download of your film, then you might receive a 30 percent royalty on that amount. It may not seem like much, but these fees can definitely add up over time. Not to mention that VOD companies license content on a nonexclusive basis, so technically you can license your movie to as many VOD companies as you like, and benefit from the royalties of all of them at once.

One advantage to distributing your film on video-on-demand platforms is that customers get to see your work right away. This helps create a buzz more quickly. And the fact that it is all online helps spread the buzz, because satisfied customers can post the URL link to your movie on various message boards and chat rooms, as well as easily email to their friends and family. You can see how, with video-on-demand distribution, word travels fast!

One disadvantage of VOD distribution is that it still isn't a big enough source of revenue to rely on for recouping the investment in your movie. Most royalty checks that I have witnessed are only a few hundred bucks per quarter, or even per year. Over time, of course, as Internet distribution becomes more and more relied upon, the economics may change. Perhaps in the future, you will be able to recoup your investment just by Internet distribution, as physical DVDs fall by the wayside. But for now, the revenue from VOD is still minuscule compared to the revenue from DVD distribution, or even theatrical distribution.

Here is a partial list of some reputable VOD companies. But keep in mind, new entities are popping up every day in this space, so be on the lookout. And remember, because all of these companies license content on a nonexclusive basis, you should absolutely license your film to as many as possible, in order to capture all of their unique audiences. Just do a little due diligence to make sure these companies actually pay the royalties that are owed to the filmmakers.

Partial List of Video-on-Demand Companies

Unbox (www.unbox.com): VOD service from CustomFlix and Amazon.com

EZTakes (www.eztakes.com): VOD service that lets you download to own movies and burn them to DVD for watching on your DVD player or computer

SpotFlix (www.spotflix.com): VOD service that rents (instead of sells) films online for a twenty-four-hour period

CinemaNow (www.cinemanow): VOD service owned by Blockbuster and Lions Gate Entertainment. They are one of the original companies pioneering VOD distribution for indies, and offering download-to-own, streaming, and download-to-burn services for customers

Google Video (www.video.google.com): The first open online video marketplace where you can set your own price—and, of course, leverage the enormous built-in Google audience

GreenCine (www.greencine.com): Independently owned and operated film addict's film site since 2002

AtomFilms (www.atomfilms.com): VOD service that specializes in short films and animations. They do not charge customers to watch films, so you will not receive any royalties. However, they do pay small advances.

Posting Your Trailer

A number of web sites allow you to post a trailer of your film, and then link back to your VOD download page or your CustomFlix page so that people can purchase your movie.

YouTube (www.youtube.com): YouTube is currently the most popular destination on the web for user-generated video content. Many filmmakers take advantage of their traffic and platform to post a promotion trailer for their film there. The sheer traffic on YouTube almost guarantees that at least a few people will be led to your other sites, where they can then download the whole film or purchase it on DVD.

Revver (www.revver.com): Revver is the first viral video network that pays content owners. For example, you upload your trailer, and they attach an unobtrusive advertisement to the end of it. When anyone clicks on the ad, you get paid.

GUBA (www.guba.com): GUBA is a leading destination for video content on the Internet, with millions of visitors watching thousands of daily updated videos.

AOL Video (www.video.aol.com): AOL Video of course benefits from all the AOL traffic, so it cannot hurt to post your trailer up here as well, in the UnCut Video upload section.

Interview with Eric Stein

Director, Content Acquisitions and Business Development
HP Digital Entertainment

What is digital rights management, and how can filmmakers benefit from it?

Digital rights management is used to protect digital content from being used in a way that would infringe on the rights of the licensor. Think of it as a combination lock around a digital file. Some distribution channels allow the consumer to download content (music, TV shows, movies) and be able to copy or move the files to other devices. Some distribution channels only allow you to watch the content on the device you downloaded it to. This is controlled by digital rights management (DRM) solutions that allow the distribution channel to dictate the rules for consumption.

There are pros and cons to DRM. This security keeps people from taking your movie and posting/distributing it on the Internet for free, or passing it around for free. If someone pays for the film, others have to also pay for the film to see it . . . like going to see a movie in a theater (i.e., each person pays to walk in the door). Without DRM, you run the risk of someone opening the theater door and allowing virtually anyone to walk in and view the movie. If your main goal is to have as large an audience as possible view the film, regardless of revenue potential, don't use DRM. If your main goal is making back your investment, you may want to consider DRM. Note that there are legal, successful services that don't use DRM—so just because you choose to not use DRM doesn't mean it will be spread around for free; you're just taking a higher risk of that happening.

Do you think the online film markets that have popped up will eventually replace AFM, MIPCOM, and all the rest of the international markets? Why or why not?
No, but the business will change a bit. The industry is based on people and connections, and this is the way business has been done for many years. This will not change overnight, but things can be more efficient when using these kinds of services. Once some companies start to see the benefits, I can easily see these companies starting to make relatively substantial changes to the ways in which this business operates. In terms of the traditional markets, it will continue to be important to see screenings, make contacts face-to-face, shake hands, and have lunch together . . . and for these reasons, I don't believe that the online marketplaces will be replacing the markets anytime soon.

Digital distribution and online film marketplaces definitely have the ability to change the business drastically over the course of the next decade, but it will all depend on how quickly the licensing community embraces this new system of doing business. The film business has been notoriously adverse to change.

What are some of the limitations to using online film markets, as opposed to signing on with a sales agent and going that route?
The main limitation right now is coverage/exposure. These services are still in the infancy stages and are not yet viable platforms for finding distribution. For them to work properly, they must bring enough of both buyers and sellers into the marketplace to make it worthwhile for both sides. It

takes time to build up a community like this, especially a community like this one, which has been doing business a certain way for many years. Sales agents typically have a good sense for who the players are, where the deals can be made, and what kinds of deals to expect. This comes from being in the business for a number of years. These online markets are just starting to scratch the surface of the community.

What do you think is the future of indie-film distribution?
Perhaps I've drank too much of the Kool-Aid, having been in digital distribution for over seven years, but I believe that over time, indie-film distribution will migrate into more distribution channels, and therefore start to find their audiences. Even now, indie-film distribution is a very small niche of product that gets very little exposure. Technology is allowing consumers to have more personalized experiences—as seen on MySpace, Facebook, and Amazon. Instead of being faced with just major megaplex movie options, consumers are seeing many more choices with the availability of digital-distribution channels. The future of indie-film distribution is immediate and democratic.

When and how do you think digital distribution will become profitable for filmmakers?
That is truly difficult to answer, as it is very broad and open-ended. My question back to you would be: "When and how do you think traditional distribution will become profitable for filmmakers?"

Bottom line: it's a tough business whether on the traditional side or new-media and digital side. I have a feeling that digital distribution is already profitable for some filmmakers—with the decreasing costs involved in actually making a film, and the decreasing costs involved in actually distributing films . . . I'm sure that some filmmakers have found ways to make a profit. I'm sure you're asking about when I think this will be the norm, or more of a reality. Truthfully, I think that over time, niche content will start to be delivered to audiences in ways that weren't possible just a few years ago. What that means in terms of profitability is hard to say.

A lot of fuss has been made about DRM, but do you think distributors/buyers are willing to embrace it totally and actually buy their products online and opt for digital delivery, as opposed to a filmmaker's having to ship a physical master?
Yes, in terms of B2B (business-to-business) application for digital distribution (i.e., digital delivery for business purposes, not straight to the con-

sumer), I think that this will very quickly become implemented and change the way this business operates internally. Shipping plastic tapes or plastic discs does not make sense when you consider the efficiencies created by digital delivery. While the technology is still a bit clunky, in the end, it makes so much more sense to send files digitally, and that goes for screeners, dailies, etc. The industry will move in that direction, but these kinds of changes take time.

As a filmmaker evaluating the online digital-distribution space, wouldn't it be easier to self-distribute on the filmmaker's web site, as opposed to giving up rights, revenues, and so on to one of the e-tailers?

No. Often filmmakers think that they can post their film on their own web site (as opposed to going with the alternatives) and keep all of the distribution revenues for themselves. While this might seem like a better choice, they forget to consider what these services have in terms of audiences/users. My advice would be to try and put the films on as many distribution outlets as possible, including their own. If you're able to put your film on Amazon, CinemaNow, Movielink, and your own web site, this is a better strategy than trying to market the film on the filmmaker's web site solely.

Online Film Markets

It is not likely that you as a filmmaker would be able to attend all of the international film and television markets to mingle with buyers and seek distribution for your film. Consequently, a perfect do-it-yourself solution for directly interacting with buyers from all over the world is to use online film markets.

With today's technology, many filmmakers find actual markets to be old-fashioned, as well as time- and money-consuming. Internet-based markets can make commerce more effective, cheaper, and faster.

Here's how it works: various online film markets have developed highly sophisticated search engines and streaming platforms that are capable of hosting an unlimited number of titles. At the click of a button, these titles can be screened online for buyers. The advanced search engines allow buyers to locate titles using multiple search vectors—from genre, format, and theme to cast and crew. Most importantly, online markets allow buyers to get a comprehensive, at-a-glance view of the available rights for each title, cross-referenced by territory.

Basically, you submit your project to the online markets, and they will create a film home page for you. You can use this home page to publicize your movie and list specific details—such as synopsis, language, cast and crew, press-kit information, upcoming showings, and so forth. Then you list your available rights for buyers to see, and of course frequently update this information as territories are sold. Finally, you get out there and market and promote your film, driving potential distributors to your site to purchase distribution rights for the territory they want.

Many filmmakers predict that a few of the Internet-based markets will become the largest year-round marketplaces for the film and television industries. Will online markets eventually replace Cannes, AFM, and all the rest? My guess is, probably not. In my opinion, there is no substitute for the exciting milieu of networking and deal making that the big markets create. But with the rapid globalization of film and television, and the almost overwhelming quantity of new products, the industry needs a parallel, year-round marketplace that provides both the capacity and convenience necessary to research, acquire, and manage rights and territories for the plethora of quality titles now available.

Here are two Internet-based film markets that are up and running:

inDplay (www.indplay.com): Currently, inDplay is the biggest player in the Internet-based film marketspace.

reelport (www.reelport.com): Through reelport, you can present your movie to potential buyers. If your film meets interest, you can either send conventional copies (for example, a screener) to the buyer, or you can provide reelport with a digital film file. With reelport, you have the potential to save on shipping costs while reaching a large audience of buyers.

Filmmaker Case Study: Bradley Beesley, on his Okie Noodling Microcinema Tour

We spent two summers lugging a 1970s CP 16mm camera through swampy creeks and snake-invested Oklahoma lakes, documenting the ancient sport of hand-fishing, otherwise known as "noodling." The result was the best two summers of my life, and a documentary movie called Okie Noodling.

We premiered Okie Noodling *to sellout crowds at the 2001 SXSW Film Festival, taking home the Audience Award for best documentary. From there, we screened at some fancy-pants festivals like Toronto International and the AFI FEST. These festivals were grandly insightful, and we actually garnered an international distribution deal in Toronto. Although festivals are fabulous exposure, they often turn into a poorly justified vacation in which you spend cash instead of making it.*

After a year on the festival circuit, I wondered if Okie Noodling *could play theatrically and make a profit. Of course, I realized no sane distribution conglomerate was going to fork over the dough for several 35mm prints and spend months promoting the film.* Okie Noodling *was funded through ITVS, and therefore my vast range of credit-card debt was only marginally obscene; so I thought . . . Why not distribute and promote the film myself? It was then that I decided to hire rock-band manager Scott Booker from the Flaming Lips, and his loyal intern, Derek Brown, to perform the bulk of the booking. Since* Okie Noodling *is not your conventional theatrical release, how would we find these art-house cinemas that would be willing to take a chance on an oddball documentary?*

By searching the Internet, it was fairly simple finding theaters that would show Okie Noodling *for one or two nights. After narrowing down our desired cities, we sent DVD screeners and press materials to theater managers, film societies, and local press. It took about two months to confirm all eight cities, with venues ranging from daily-operating 700-person theaters to small record stores. In the end, we had successfully booked a movie tour. Our plan was to attend the screening in each city, allowing time for Q&A and merchandise sales.*

Basement Films in Albuquerque, New Mexico, was the first stop. This nomadic underground-film series has a dedicated following and warmly eccentric members. We set up a seventies-style video projector in a record store in front of an enthusiastic sold-out crowd of 50. Our guarantee of 150 bucks was met, and later that night Keith from Basement Films gave us a guided tour through the maze of wonderful 16 mm films.

Our next screening was in San Francisco at the fiercely independent ATA, or Artists' Television Access. Things picked up, as we sold out the house of 100. Additionally, we showed a seven-minute work in progress from the Flaming Lips sci-fi-narrative Christmas on Mars.

In Portland [Oregon], I felt our tour had really begun as we pulled up to the historic Hollywood Theatre (a 1920s vaudevillian cinema) and Okie Noodling *was bolstered on the marquee. We had two screenings for more than 200 cheering spectators and sold plenty of merchandise.*

The crowd grew to 250 in Olympia, Washington, at the impressive Capitol Theater run by Sean Savage and the Olympia Film Society. Unfortunately, we didn't allow time to test the projector before the house lights went down. After two minutes of the film, we had to stop the projector and apologize to the confused crowd, and explain that I wasn't sure what they had just seen, but it was certainly not my movie, as the hue, contrast, and saturation were whacked. Luckily, the crowd understood, and responded well with a heated Q&A. Before heading north for Seattle, we once again pilfered our VHS tapes and T-shirts for a nice sum.

The Experience Music Project in Seattle was our next stop. The JBL surround-sound cinema was amazing. Okie Noodling *has never looked nor sounded so grand. We also screened our thirty-minute documentary* The Flaming Lips Have Landed, *and the 185-person theater was standing room only.*

Next up was Boise, Idaho. This screening was going to be in what was usually a rock-club venue, and I wasn't anticipating a large crowd. I gave my customary cell-phone call to the venue five hours before showtime to confirm the details. Much to my surprise, they had changed the screening time from 10 p.m. to 8 p.m. and forgotten to notify us. Due to the weather, we would be lucky to even make it to the scheduled 10 p.m. screening. They compromised and started the movie at 9 p.m. without us. Unfortunately, we got pulled over by the fuzz and showed up as the credits were rolling. I bolted onstage, grabbed the mic, and proceeded with the Q&A

to a rowdy and insightful crowd of 150. Meanwhile, my travel partner and co-Okie producer, Mr. Damon Cook, proceeded to sell $680 in merchandise—the most to date. Thank you, Boise!

We had to turn away 50 people in Salt Lake City, and had our third sellout of the tour. There was a fifteen-minute delay due to lack of sound, but the crackerjack staff at Brewvies managed to empty the 175-person cinema and magically corrected the audio nightmare. Once we corralled the raucous audience back in the theater, they sat mesmerized for sixty minutes and seemed to thoroughly enjoy the noodling experience.

Last on our eight-city adventure was the sleepy ski town of Durango, Colorado, at the Abbey Theatre. It was only a twelve-hour stay in Durango, but the audience of 100 was giddy. I have yet to hear so many people laugh, clap, and awe during a screening of Okie Noodling. Maybe it was the Colorado kind bud?

In the end, we traveled through twelve states, put 5,500 miles on our "tristate" rental car, busted the transmission, drove through a grass fire, and ultimately screened Okie Noodling to over 1,600 enthusiastic fans. It was absolutely an experience of a lifetime; and in the end, we made over $2,300 after expenses.

In the days of the super-mega-multiplex twenty-four movie theater/shopping mall craze, it's heartening to know there remain a few brave souls who support independent cinemas and alternative theaters in America.

Art-house Cinemas at Which My Films Have Screened

Alamo Drafthouse Cinema (Austin, Tex.)
www.drafthouse.com
Aurora Picture Show (Houston)
www.aurorapictureshow.org
Brattle Theatre (Cambridge, Mass.)
www.brattlefilm.org
Cable Car Cinema & Café (Providence, R.I.)
www.cablecarcinema.com
Capri Theatre (Montgomery, Ala.)
capritheatre.org

Enzian Theater (Maitland, Fla.)
www.enzian.org
Fargo Theatre (Fargo, N.Dak.)
www.fargotheatre.org
The Flicks (Boise, Idaho)
www.theflicksboise.com
Hollywood Theatre (Portland, Ore.)
www.hollywoodtheatre.org
Minnesota Film Arts (Minneapolis)
www.mnfilmarts.org
Northwest Film Center (Portland, Ore.)
www.nwfilm.org
Orpheum Theatre (Madison, Wis.)
www.orpheumtheatre.net
Pioneer Theater (New York City)
www.twoboots.com/pioneer
Red Vic Movie House (San Francisco)
www.redvicmoviehouse.com

Platform Theatrical Release

If you want to release your film theatrically in do-it-yourself fashion, you can go the route of many filmmakers these days and do a platform theatrical release.

With this approach, you release your film in one or two local theaters, start to generate significant buzz, and then slowly and strategically release the picture in additional theaters. The ultimate goal is that one of the big distributors takes notice, buys the film out from you, and gives it a wide release.

A platform theatrical release normally requires raising additional capital—you'll need both prints and sufficient advertising to get booked into a theater. For example, you approach a theater owner to see if they will book your film for a weekend. Their typical response will be to require you to show them proof that you have purchased advertising in local newspapers. This is to ensure that there is at least a minimum guarantee that people will show up to see your movie. Booking a theater for a weekend is precious real estate for a theater owner. In order for them to take the risk with your film, they will definitely want to know your plan for driving ticket sales.

If you can prove yourself to theater owners, they will agree to book your picture for a weekend. If the film does good weekend numbers, the theater will extend you another week. If your film does good numbers for another week, they will extend you again. And so on.

Conversely, if your movie happens to tank that opening weekend, by Monday it will be removed. I've seen this happen many times with pictures that have impressive casts but just couldn't garner an audience. So keep in mind, the key with a platform theatrical release is to keep it going—and to keep it going, you have to market your film as hard as you possibly can. Get creative and start early. Hire a publicist. Get press and interviews and do guerrilla marketing to your core audience. You have to do whatever you can to drive ticket sales.

Of course, if you have a traditional distributor for your project, these are all the things they would handle—but they would be under the same pressure as you to sell tickets. And if your film doesn't sell tickets, it will be out of the theaters after one weekend, even if you have a big distributor behind you. When it comes to ticket sales, the theater owners do not discriminate.

Ultimately, if you have the resources to go the route of a platform theatrical release, I strongly encourage it. This might just give you the "bump" you need to get noticed by a major distributor.

Keep in mind that if you decide to open your film in one of the bigger markets (New York, Los Angeles), it will cost significantly more money, and you will be competing with numerous other movies for viewers. Alternatively, if you open in a smaller market, advertising costs will be cheaper, and viewers may consider you a welcome alternative to studio fare.

If you don't have money left in your budget to do a platform theatrical release, you can hire an independent sales rep to do sales projections and a cash-flow statement for you. You could then use the sales projections and cash-flow statement to raise the necessary capital from investors. The point is that having a U.S. theatrical release raises the value of your film internationally, thus opening up international sales potential. However, I will say that from personal experience, international buyers will want to know how many theaters the picture was released in, what the gross ticket sales were, and so on. It's not enough to just say your movie had a theatrical release. You really need to put the marketing muscle behind it to make your picture successful enough to grow "legs" and spread to more theaters in your market, and then to additional markets.

For example, I was working with a filmmaker who had a very well produced independent film, complete with an A-list movie star and a very popular TV star. So far, so good. We decided to do a platform theatrical release, and began marketing the project about four months prior to the release. We got a national television interview, several radio interviews, and blurbs in a couple of major magazines. We also paid for advertising in the major newspapers and purchased billboards. We even had a huge premiere party. There was tremendous buzz for this little picture.

The film opened up in one theater in Los Angeles—and even with all the marketing and advertising behind the picture, there were hardly any ticket sales. After only one weekend, the movie was dropped. That's the danger of opening in L.A. or any of the other big markets. The bigger the market, the more competition for your picture. Our film had all the right ingredients for success, but no ticket sales to back it up.

In any case, we took all the press the movie had garnered, and used that publicity to put together quite an impressive press kit. I used the press kit to try and make international sales of the film. I screened the well-made trailer for buyers, showed the press kit, and touted the fact that the picture had enjoyed a U.S. theatrical release. The first thing the buyers asked me was how many theaters and what were the gross ticket sales. Once they found out the movie had been in only one theater for one weekend, they weren't interested.

The moral of the story? If you can pull together a platform theatrical release for your film, great. However, as I said before, make sure you not only market the daylights out of your project to get people to come and see it, but also that you seriously consider the market in which you're opening. Another thing: if you're borrowing more money from investors to make the platform release happen, be up front with them about the odds. Unless your film is a sellout success in your first few theaters, it will never make it to other theaters and markets—which is where your investors' money would be recouped.

On a more positive note, I want to share with you my favorite platform theatrical release success story by far in the past few years.

The producers of *What the Bleep Do We Know!?* had made a picture that appealed to a niche audience. Knowing this, they made sure to put aside enough money for marketing to this niche audience. As a result, their movie went on to do a very successful platform theatrical release. The producers first released the film for one weekend in a theater in their hometown. After making sure that every screening was sold out, they platformed the movie like this in city after city—until Samuel Goldwyn Films stepped in, bought the picture, took it out wide, and released it on DVD.

Interview with Betsy Chasse, producer of indie success *What the Bleep Do We Know!?*

Did you have a distribution strategy in mind when you made the film? Were you thinking theatrical release, straight-to-DVD, or just go with the flow?
We hoped we would either get into a film festival or that a distributor would pick up the film.

I understand you opened the film theatrically starting in just one theater in a small market, and then "platformed" it from there to more theaters and bigger markets. Did you put aside money in your initial budget for prints and advertising? Or did you raise additional money after the film was shot? How much would you recommend filmmakers set aside to do an effective platform release of their film?

Will Arntz financed the film himself. We initially hoped a distributor would pay for the release, but once it was obvious that wasn't going to happen, Will put up the P&A [prints and advertising money] *himself.*

How much would you recommend filmmakers set aside to do an effective platform release of their film?
It depends on them. If they know their audience and can muster a good grassroots campaign to gain word of mouth, they don't need much. It's not until you start hitting thirty or forty theaters that it starts adding up. Also, with a good grassroots campaign, you can avoid the expensive mainstream newspapers. Eventually, to break out, you'll need them— but until then, use the Internet and other grassroots campaigns to get the word out.

Did you do all of the theater booking yourselves? Did you find the theater owners were supportive of your plan?
I booked the first twenty theaters myself. In the beginning, our first theater was supportive. But I knew the owners. The second theater gave us a shot—but didn't expect much—they were pleasantly surprised. We played there for over twenty weeks. After about the fourth theater where our grassroots and word-of-mouth campaign had been really working, theaters and bookers started calling me. I was able at that point to make a deal with a couple of big chains, which immediately doubled our screens.

I read an article that all of your initial showings were sold out. That's amazing—and the theater owners must have been thrilled! How did you do it?
As I mentioned before: grassroots . . . Internet . . . really knowing our audience and how to find them. We did seed screenings and special screenings for opinion makers. Word of mouth was huge before we opened our second theater.

How many initial prints did you make, and what was your advertising strategy?
We started with two prints and ended with about 150. Our advertising strategy was independent alternative, Internet and radio shows, which fed our core audience. We had done market research. We knew which shows, magazines, and press would write about us and whose audience would want to hear about the film.

Did you choose to go the festival route before platform releasing the film yourselves? Why or why not?
We did—but it didn't really affect anything. My feeling is that the festival market has been so saturated and overtaken by studio "independent" that most of the true independents don't make it through. If you are outside of the movie industry, do you know who won Sundance last year? I would enter—but have an alternative plan. Also, save money by holding off on doing a film out [finishing on film] and making prints—many theaters can project digitally. Also, look into alternative venues. The idea is for people to see your film. That doesn't mean it has to be in a theater. The old model is ready to be broken. We do special screenings with DVD projectors, which look great in churches, colleges, etc. It also makes you more money to expand your film. You cut out the middlemen (bookers, theaters, distributors). Once your film has enough buzz, then you are in a better position to negotiate with them.

Did you try and place the film with foreign-sales agents? Why or why not?
We waited until the film was doing well in the market. We had such a niche film that we had to prove its worthiness before we could talk to foreign buyers.

At what point did you start getting approached by big distributors to acquire the film? Whom did you choose to go with, and why?
*Once the film hit about $2 million and twenty screens. Actually, we would have continued to do it ourselves, except I was about three weeks away from giving birth to my first child and became overwhelmed. We had requests coming in from all over the country. We went with Goldwyn because of their success with **Super Size Me**, and we liked them. We had offers from studios, but felt that we could continue the successful marketing plan we had created by keeping it with a smaller company. We also hired a marketing company to continue the marketing strategy and work on getting us into the bigger media.*

As you are aware, it is becoming more and more difficult to get a U.S. theatrical distribution deal these days. Do you have any advice for filmmakers who want to take the road you did, and platform release their movie themselves?
Go for it. There is no reason you can't do it. Whether you have $500 or $5 million. Start small and let it build. The "slow burn" is a good thing. It lets the word of mouth spread, and people go nuts for things they can't

have! Make them wait a bit. Also, you can grow your bank account to get you more and more exposure. Also, it's a great "proof of concept" for distributors, etc. Once they see it can work, they'll want it, and you'll be in the driver's seat in the deal.

Looking back, is there anything you would have done differently? If so, why?
Nope. I had never released a film theatrically myself, nor had anyone on my team. We just figured it out as we went along, and I think we did a pretty good job. Thanks to Pavel, Melissa, and Gabby, we were a five-person distribution company (including Will and myself) before we took on more help. And we grossed $2 million on twenty screens—so it doesn't take a lot of people. It takes dedication and a passion for your project.

Hybrid Distribution Model

There is a hybrid distribution model that is starting to take shape. This model combines three elements: (1) a self-distribution platform theatrical release, (2) traditional DVD distribution, and (3) online DVD distribution rights carved out for the filmmaker.

For example, if you make a film that doesn't immediately get distribution, you may choose to do your own platform theatrical release, the way Betsy Chasse did with *What the Bleep Do We Know!?* While you're doing your own platform theatrical release, you may decide to sell your own DVDs at the screenings, the way Bradley Beesley did with *Okie Noodling*. At this point, you will probably also want to sell DVDs from your web site or your CustomFlix site, to capitalize on the fact that you are out there creating a buzz doing public screenings. With all this in place, you are completely self-distributed.

Suddenly, a traditional DVD distributor picks up on all the buzz you're getting, and sees that there is a market for your product, and that you are actually selling DVDs, and they want in on the action! *But* . . . you have a nice successful online operation going, and you don't want to give up that revenue. After all, for every DVD you sell from your own web site, you could be pocketing between $5 and $15, depending on the selling price of the DVD.

Once a DVD distributor picks up your film, you might make $2 to $3 per unit sold, at most.

So you are left with a conundrum. Whereas you always wanted a DVD distributor to offer you a deal, you also are enjoying the revenue that you're making while self-distributing. The perfect solution is to negotiate in your contract with the distributor that you, the filmmaker, retain online-distribution rights to your film. This would have been unheard of a few years ago, but surprisingly, DVD distributors are realizing that they have to acquiesce in this area if they want to be able to acquire hot-performing niche films that are already out there collecting a buzz in the marketplace. Distributors are also realizing that a filmmaker who is heavily promoting a movie online will only help their retail sales in the long run anyway. So everybody wins.

I interviewed distribution strategist Peter Broderick, one of the industry pioneers of this concept. Peter contends that distributors don't have a choice anymore; rather, they absolutely have to alter their business models to accommodate filmmakers in this area. Traditional DVD distributors will be more like retail partners in the future, and filmmakers will leverage the new technologies available to them and handle their own online distribution.

Another part of the hybrid distribution model that Peter has been instrumental in popularizing is known as "house parties." Some filmmakers are taking their platform theatrical release to art-house and independent movie theaters. Meanwhile, others are choosing to do targeted screenings—house parties—in people's homes.

A great example of this model is Robert Greenwald's *Wal-Mart: The High Cost of Low Price*. Robert really wanted to get his message out there, and knew how to find his target audience online. By galvanizing online support, he organized grassroots screenings at people's homes all across the country. This built a tremendous buzz for his film. Robert ended up having somewhere around a thousand house parties, each with ten to fifteen people in a living room. Within a couple of months, he had sold a hundred thousand DVDs to people who bought them at the parties and from his web site.

Granted, the house-party strategy works very well with documentaries that lend themselves to strong grassroots opinions and campaigns—*but* you could also apply this strategy to a narrative feature if your film appeals to a core audience (e.g., surfers, teenagers, sports enthusiasts . . . whatever). Think about what groups people belong to online and how you can reach them. Then capitalize on that enthusiasm and organize screenings around it.

It almost makes sense these days to think in terms of what types of films could appeal to what groups online, and work backward from there. At least that way, you will always have the insurance of direct sales of your DVD online, and know that you'll be able to make online revenue to pay back your investors. Even if a traditional distributor never picks up your film, you know you can do some grassroots promoting and selling all on your own.

Something else to think about is that while you're out there doing grassroots screenings, building an audience for yourself, you may well be able to raise money for your next project. I know of a few filmmakers who, while showing their movies to a targeted demographic at private screenings, met investors who were interested in financing future projects. So keep your eyes open and be prepared!

Suggested Exercises for Part Eight

1. Sketch out your online-distribution plan. What does it look like, and what is the timeline for everything?
2. Post your trailer (or short video) to one of the web sites mentioned above. Link it to your web site. What kind of traffic are you seeing? And what can you do to increase the traffic and build buzz?
3. Call a local theater in your town or another city, and ask the theater owner what the requirements are for getting your film in for a theatrical release. This is practice in case you want to go with a do-it-yourself platform theatrical release. Familiarize yourself with the requirements for advertising, film format for projecting, fees involved, and so on.

4. Do some realistic sales projections for your picture based on a self-distribution plan. Include on-demand DVD distribution, online distribution, and a platform theatrical release.

My Very Best Advice to You

I have already covered ways that will help you find distribution for your film. As my parting words, I'll give you a few final tips.

First, it's important to have a good lawyer. I can give you all the advice in the world and fully educate you about the process of distribution; however, I cannot read your individual contracts. I can explain standard contracts in detail and tell you what to look out for, what's normal, and what may be suspect (please see bonus section for this), but I cannot fully scrutinize each contract and make sure you have negotiated the best deal available. For this, you need a lawyer. An attorney will scrutinize your contract and make sure everything is in order and on the up-and-up.

Second, remember that film is a collaborative medium. When you start working on a movie, you're in it for the long haul. The process of filmmaking does not end on the last day of post. The picture may be with you for years afterward while going through the distribution process, and you will need to take along several people on the journey. Even the truest auteur cannot do it alone. You are entrusting your film—and quite possibly your future—to certain individuals, and it is extremely important to build a team of collaborators you trust. These are people you may be working with for years, so carefully pick and choose whom you want to be working with, spending time with, and, most importantly, entrusting your film to.

Third, we all know that making a movie is hard work. Getting someone to buy that picture and put it out there for audiences the world over often can be even harder work. In some cases, you may find yourself in the following scenario: you've got a well-made, marketable film; you've considered the realities of distribution; you've gotten positive feedback from buyers and maybe even a few audiences—but you still have no sales. Please don't give up.

As I've said before, the market is a fickle place. Keep in mind that your work may be in a genre that isn't selling at the moment, or it may fall into a genre that's been temporarily oversaturated. If you pay close attention to what's selling at any given time, you will see that the market is a cycle. For a few months, closely follow what's selling, You'll begin to see a pattern develop. If you have a comedy that isn't selling, hold tight and try to market it again at a time when comedies are hot. You may get a bite then. If you've got a thriller, a drama, a horror flick, or a film that falls into any other category, the same holds true. If you hold out just a little longer and wait for the market to come around, your luck may change.

The nature of the marketplace demands a heavy saturation of one or two genres at any given time. This strategy promotes healthy competition at the box office between distributors. Once there is a perceived oversaturation of a given genre, the cycle advances, and so on and so forth. Ever notice how a bunch of westerns all seem to hit theaters at once and then vanish? Or costume dramas? Or teen gross-out comedies? There's a reason. Distributors are in fierce competition with each other. So if you happen to hit at the wrong time, remember that you may just be hitting at the wrong time—a few months down the road, things could be very different. That is just another reality of the marketplace.

Appendix A

Anatomy of a Distribution Agreement

In this bonus section, I have dissected a typical distribution agreement between producer and sales agent/rep. This is an invaluable tool for understanding what the rep will ask of you, before going into business with them.

In this section, I've given you a general overview of what will be presented to you in the distribution agreement. However, this is by no means comprehensive—each company and/or rep will tailor this basic agreement to best suit their needs. So the actual agreement may contain additional sections that are not presented here. Also, some things that are presented here may not appear in the actual agreement. Please note that once you choose a rep or company you wish to work with, and you begin the actual negotiation process of the contract, do consult a lawyer to let you know exactly what you're signing up for and to work out the finer points.

My goal here is simply to break it all down for you, in plain English (not all the legalese you'll eventually be faced with). I want to prepare you for what will be demanded of you in a contract, and offer suggestions on what to ask for and how to make the terms more in your favor.

The Terms

I. Name, Company Name, and Territory:

Be sure to use the name and address of your company—or, if you have one, the name and address of your limited-liability corporation.

The sales rep will refer to themselves as "distributor" for purposes of the contract. Realize that you are signing an agreement with them to sell your film to other distributors (such as DVD companies, television networks, and theatrical distributors).

Be alert to what territory the sales rep is trying to claim. If you agreed on "U.S. rights only," then be sure that the agreement indicates this—and not, for example, "North American rights." Also, be very cautious in signing away worldwide rights of your film. Don't give these rights to just anyone—you want to have seriously considered the rep, checked their references, and followed all the other advice I gave you earlier.

II. Term

It is customary to say that the term of the contract is "for seven years after complete delivery of all materials set forth in Delivery Materials List." First thing to note is that a rep will ask for at least a five- or seven-year term, and may ask for as much as a fifteen-year term. The reason they need at least a five-year term is because the distributors to whom they sell your film will demand at least a five-year term—so the rep needs to show that they have the rights to sell your film for that amount of time.

Why does a distributor need as long a term as possible? Because it takes several years for them to recoup the marketing and other expenses they invest in your film.

Regarding the term of your contract with the rep, it is to your advantage to negotiate the least amount of years possible. That way, if you are unhappy with the rep's performance, you can get out sooner rather than later, and have the rights to your film revert back to you.

III. Exclusive Grant of Rights

It is important to note that during the term of the contract, whether it's five or fifteen years or whatever, you do not own the rights to your film. If, at any point during this term, you are approached directly by a distributor, you are contractually obligated to refer the sale to your rep so that they can execute the sale and earn their commission. Now, to clarify completely, this is only in regard to any territory you have sold off to a rep. For example, if you have an agreement in place for only the United States, you are still free to sell the film in England, provided that territory remains unrepresented with regard to your project.

IV. Distributor's Fee

As I mentioned earlier, a rep will take a commission of between 10 and 30 percent. Most common is 25 percent. These fees are taken "off the top" of each sale. What this means is that when the revenue from a sale comes in (moneys will be wired to their account, not yours), the rep takes their fee first, and then calculates the balance as owed to you.

Obviously, it is to your advantage to negotiate as low a distributor's fee as possible. Independent sales reps are more likely to accept a lower commission, because they do not have the same overheads as bigger sales agencies do. The large agencies will most likely not budge on their commission. In my opinion, all sales reps definitely earn their commission. In most cases, they are able to get a much higher price than you could have on your own. So don't sweat this part too much.

V. Distributor's Expenses

You definitely want to pay close attention to this section of the contract! This is where the rep states that they will be able to re-coup from "producer's share of gross receipts" all of the rep's out-of-pocket servicing, marketing, publicity, promotion, delivery, distribution and any other customary expenses paid or incurred by the distributor in connection with your movie. What this means is that before the sales rep begins paying you revenues from the sales of your film, they have the right to first recoup an agreed-upon amount (normally between $10,000 and $50,000) before they start sharing profits with you. The Catch-22 is that with licensing fees so low out there, it normally takes several years before the sales rep recoups their expenses, if ever. I say "if ever" because I have seen many, many cases where the producer never actually sees any revenue from the sales of his or her film, because the sales rep never actually accrues enough in licensing fees. For example, if the sales rep makes, say, five sales to DVD distributors in small territories (which is very common for an independent film with no stars), that could amount to as little as $10,000 in revenue. You will not see this revenue—the distributor takes it as part of expenses. However, once additional sales are made that exceed the $30,000 mark, the distributor will pay you 75 percent (or whatever percentage has been agreed upon) of every dollar of every sale.

Many people question whether or not sales reps actually rack up that much money in expenses, thus deserving to keep the first $30,000 in sales of a film before paying out to producers. Without a doubt, the distributor will incur expenses. Just think of how much it costs to design campaigns, print flyers and posters, ship screening cassettes, and go to all the international film markets. Then think of how much this would amount to when amortized over the term of the contract. In most cases, the sales rep breaks even with expenses. In some unfortunate cases, however, they will "gouge" the filmmaker by putting a ridiculously high number in the contract, hoping the filmmaker doesn't notice or doesn't fully understand the process. In my opinion, anything over $30,000 for an independent film without a theatrical release is a ridiculously high number.

VI. Producer's Share of Remaining Gross Receipts

This section explains that from each sale, the rep first takes their fee (normally 25 percent), followed by recoupment of any expenses.

Thereafter, from all remaining gross receipts, 75 percent will be paid to the producer.

Here is how this works. Say that the rep makes a sale to a distributor for $10,000. It is the first sale they've made. Per the contract, they are allowed to recoup $30,000 in marketing expenses. This means that the rep would claim $2,500 as their fee, and keep the balance of $7,500 toward the $30,000 in expenses they are allowed to claim.

Now, say that they make a second sale for $25,000. From this second sale, they keep $6,250 as their fee, and the balance of $18,750 goes toward their marketing expenses. So far, in $35,000 in sales of your film, the distributor has made $8,750 in distribution fees, and has recouped $26,250 toward their $30,000 in marketing expenses. Meanwhile, you have made nothing . . . yet.

O.K., so now the rep makes a third sale for $15,000. They take their fee of $3,750, with another $3,750 to reach their $30,000 in expenses—and now you get the balance of $7,500. From every sale here on out, the distributor will take only their 25 percent fee, and give you the rest (now that they have recouped their $30,000 in marketing expenses).

VII. Delivery of the Picture

This section explains that until you deliver all the elements listed in the Delivery Schedule portion of the contract, the sales rep is not obligated to begin making sales of your film. In fact, until you've delivered all the appropriate materials, it is actually difficult for them to start making sales. Here's a typical list of materials that you can expect to have to deliver. Please note, there may be more (or fewer) items, depending on the rep.

1. Digibeta master or Betacam SP w/certified QC (quality check) report from your lab
2. (20) Slides (in slide format or on disc)
3. Publicity
4. Synopsis
5. Music cue sheet

6. Dialogue script
7. Bonus materials
8. Trailer
9. Chain of title verification (i.e., copyright)
10. E&O (errors and omissions) insurance certificate
11. M&E (music and effects) tracks

You have to understand that the reson the rep will be so strict about collecting these deliverables from you is not because they are trying to be difficult (although it will seem like that!); rather, it's because the distributors to whom they sell will demand each and every one of these items—maybe even *more*. I know some distributors who use this tactic to hold up payment. For example, on several occasions, I've made sales to DVD companies whereby I deliver the master, M&E tracks, artwork, dialogue script, and so on—but when I invoice for payment, the distributor will come back to me and say they won't pay until I provide them with an E&O insurance certificate. It doesn't matter that we both know that they don't need the E&O certificate until they actually release the film six months hence. No, they will absolutely not pay the deposit until each and every item on the list is delivered. This allows them to hold on to their cash much longer—they know how difficult (and oftentimes expensive) it is for independent filmmakers to get all these materials together.

VIII. Accounting Records and Audit Rights

In this section, you want to make sure that the sales rep has to account to you every quarter. It is in their interest to account to you fewer times a year than every quarter—in fact, they will probably push for once a year—but try to get them to agree to quarterly accounting statements. This allows you to keep better tabs on what sales are taking place. Also, when you start getting revenue checks, you'll get them four times a year rather than once.

Additionally, this section explains that you have the right, at your expense, to audit the sales rep or sales company once a year. That way, if you suspect that anything fishy is going on, or if you aren't getting straight answers regarding sales of your film and payments, then you can hire an independent third party to look into the matter.

IX. Default

In my opinion, this is the most important part of the contract. Basically, it states that if either party violates terms of the contract, the other party has the right to explain in writing how terms are being violated. Then, if the other party doesn't make amends, the contract can be canceled. What this means to you is that you have an "out"—should you ever want or need one.

For example, suppose that the rep fails to send you accounting statements on a quarterly basis (or whatever has been agreed upon). In that case, you should notify them, in writing, that they are violating terms of the contract. If, after thirty days, they still fail to produce an accounting report for you, you have the right to cancel the contract—at which point the rights to your film would revert back to you, and you could request the return of your masters, and so on and so forth.

Of course, the Default section works both ways. If you, the producer, fail to deliver all the materials defined in the contract (and believe me, this is often the most challenging part of getting into business with a rep), then the rep or sales company has the right to give you, in writing, thirty days to deliver all the required elements. Then if you, after having received this notice, don't come up with everything, they can cancel the contract—and give you back your film for you to deal with on your own.

Appendix B

Sample U.S. Distribution Contract

Agreement made and entered into as of May 1, 2006, by and between hereby known as Distributor [Enter address, telephone, fax, email. Production company] and hereby known as Producer [Enter address, telephone, fax, email]. In consideration of their respective covenants, warranties, and representations, together with other good and valuable consideration, Distributor and Producer hereby agree as follows:

I. PICTURE: Producer will deliver to Distributor the documentation, advertising, and physical materials (the "Materials") set forth in the attached Delivery Schedule (Exhibit "A"), relating to the motion picture with the running time of 80 minutes currently entitled: Enter title of film.

II. RIGHTS GRANTED:

A. Producer hereby grants to Distributor the irrevocable, right, title, and interest in and to the distribution of the Picture, its sound, and music, in the Territory (as hereinafter defined), including, without limitation, the sole, exclusive, and irrevocable right and privilege, under Producer's copyright and otherwise, to distribute, license, and otherwise exploit the Picture, its image, sound, and music (as embodied in the Picture only) during the Term (as hereinafter defined) throughout the Territory (as hereinafter defined) for Home Video/DVD,

Video On Demand (VOD), and Internet (collectively, the "Media"). Such rights do not include the rights to produce other motion pictures, or sequels, or remakes of the Picture, or any right to produce television series, miniseries, or programs or the rights to license clips from the Picture or other so-called ancillary rights (herein called "Reserved Rights"). Without limiting the generality of the foregoing, or any other rights granted to Distributor elsewhere in this Agreement, Producer •• the following rights:

1. Home Video/DVD Rights: All rights in and to the manufacture, distribution, exploitation, and nontheatrical, nonadmission, free home-use exhibition of the Picture, its sound, and music (whether by sale or by rental), by means of any and all forms of videocassette, videodisc, video cartridge, tape, memory cards, or other similar device ("Videogram") now known or hereafter devised and designed to be used in conjunction with a reproduction apparatus which causes a visual image (whether or not synchronized with sound) to be seen on the screen of a television receiver, personal computer, personal handheld device (e.g., phone, PDA), or any comparable device now known or hereafter devised, including DVD (the "Home Video Rights" or "Video Rights" or "DVD Rights").

2. Video On Demand (VOD) and Internet: All rights in and to the distribution, exhibition, marketing, and other exploitation of the Picture, its sound, and music by means of "Internet" & "Video On Demand" as that expression is commonly understood in the motion picture industry.

B. Advertising: Distributor shall have the exclusive right throughout the Territory during the Term to advertise and publicize (or have its subdistributors advertise and publicize) the Picture by any and all means, media, and method whatsoever, including by means of the distribution, exhibition, broadcasting, and telecasting of trailers of the Picture, or excerpts from the Picture prepared by Distributor or others, subject to any customary restrictions upon and obligations with respect to such rights as are provided for in the contracts in relation to the production of the Picture.

C. Title: Distributor shall have the right to use the present title of the Picture.

D. Distributor may add its own logo/branding/advertising to the packaging, advertising materials, and at the end or beginning of the Picture. Additionally, Distributor may add a "ghost logo" superimposed on Picture.

E. Licensing: Distributor has the right to grant licenses and other authorizations to one or more third parties to exercise any or all of said rights and privileges provided herein, for any and all territories throughout the Territory.

III. RESERVED RIGHTS: All other rights not expressly written herein, including, but not limited to, electronic publishing, print publication, music publishing, live-television, radio, and dramatic rights, are reserved to the Producer.

IV. TERRITORY: The Territory (herein "Territory") for which rights are granted to Distributor consists of The World.

V. TERM: The rights granted to Distributor under this Agreement will commence on the date of delivery to Distributor of all delivery items listed in Delivery Items (Exhibit "A"), and continue thereafter for nine (9) years ("Initial Term"). This Agreement will thereafter renew automatically for successive three (3)-year periods (each, a "Renewal Term"), unless either party notifies the other in writing at least thirty (30) days prior to the end of the Initial Term or any Renewal Term that it does not wish to renew. If such notification is given by either party, this Agreement will remain in full effect for a one (1)-year "transition period" after the end of the then-current Term, to allow both parties time to make alternate arrangements. Exception: If Producer has not received fifty thousand dollars ($50,000) prior to the end of the fourth year (during the "Initial Term"), Producer may terminate this Agreement by written notice to Distributor, thirty (30) days prior to the fourth-year anniversary of this contract.

VI. ADVERTISING: Producer will supply to Distributor advertising and marketing materials as set forth on the attached Delivery Schedule (Exhibit "A").

VII. COPYRIGHT: Producer represents and warrants that the Picture is, and will be throughout the Term, protected by copyright. Each copy of the Picture will contain a copyright notice conforming to and complying with the most current requirements of the United States Copyright Act.

VIII. PRODUCTION COSTS: As between Producer and Distributor: Producer is and will be responsible for and has paid or will pay all production costs, taxes, fees, and charges with respect to the Picture and/or the Materials, except as provided herein. As used herein, "production costs" will include all costs incurred in connection with the production of the Picture and the Materials, including payments to writers, producers, directors, artists, and all other persons rendering services in connection with the Picture and/or the materials, all costs and expenses incurred in acquiring rights to use music in connection with the Picture, including synchronization, performance, and mechanical reproduction fees and union residuals.

IX. PRODUCER'S REPRESENTATION AND WARRANTIES: Producer warrants and represents to Distributor, to the best of Producer's knowledge and belief, as follows:

A. Producer has full right, power, and authority to enter into and perform this Agreement and to grant to Distributor all of the rights herein granted and agreed to be granted hereunder.

B. Producer has acquired, or will have acquired prior to the delivery of the Picture hereunder, and will maintain during the Term all rights in and to the literary and musical material upon which the Picture is based or which are used therein, and any other rights necessary and required for the exploitation of the Picture, as permitted hereunder.

C. Producer will state that neither the Picture nor the Materials nor any part thereof, nor any literary, dramatic, or musical works or any other materials contained therein or synchronized therewith, nor the exercise of any right, license, or privilege herein granted, violates or will violate, or infringes or will infringe, any trademark, trade name, contract, agreement, copyright (whether common law or statutory), patent literary, artistic, dramatic, personal, private, civil, or property right or right of privacy or "moral right of author," or any law or regulation or other right whatsoever of, or slanders or libels, any person, firm, corporation, or association.

D. Producer has not sold, assigned, transferred, or conveyed, and will not sell, assign, transfer, or convey, to any party, any right, title, or interest in and to the Picture or any part thereof, or in and to the dramatic, musical, or literary material upon which it is based, adverse to or derogatory of or which would interfere with the rights granted to Distributor, and has not and will not authorize any other party to exercise any right or take any action which will derogate from the rights herein granted or purported to be granted to Distributor.

E. Producer will obtain and maintain all necessary licenses for the production, exhibition, performance, distribution, marketing, and exploitation of the Picture and/or the Materials, including, without limitation, the synchronization and performance of all music contained therein, throughout the Territory during the Term for any and all purposes contemplated hereunder. Producer further represents and warrants that as between the Producer and Distributor, the performing rights to all musical compositions contained in the Picture and/or the Materials will be controlled by Producer to the extent required for the purposes of the Agreement, and that no payments will be required to be made by Distributor to any third party for the use of such music in the Materials or on television or in Videogram embodying the Picture (or, if any such music payments are required, Producer will be solely responsible therefore).

F. Producer represents and warrants all artists, actors, musicians, and persons rendering services in connection with the production of the Picture or the materials have been or will be paid by Producer the sums required to be paid to them under applicable agreements, and the sums required to be paid pursuant to any applicable pension or similar trusts (e.g., WGA, DGA, SAG, AFTRA) required thereby will be made by Producer, in a due and timely manner.

G. Producer warrants that the Picture and Advertising Materials and Distributor's use thereof do not and will not

1. infringe upon or violate any copyright, trademark, trade name, trade secret, patent, moral right, literary, artistic, dramatic, contract, or other intellectual or proprietary or other right of any third party;

2. infringe upon the right of privacy or publicity of any person;

3. constitute a libel or slander of any person;

4. violate any applicable law, statute, ordinance, or regulation; or

5. be deemed to be obscene or pornographic. Producer has not been charged or threatened with infringement or violation of any intellectual property or other right of any person or entity in connection with the Picture or Advertising Materials. The Picture and Advertising Materials do not and will not contain any defects, viruses, worms, Trojan horses, date bombs, time bombs, or other harmful components.

X. DISTRIBUTOR'S WARRANTIES: Distributor warrants that it is solvent and not in danger of bankruptcy. Distributor has the authority to enter into this Agreement, and there are and, to the best of Distributor's knowledge and belief, will be, no claims, actions, suits, arbitrations, or other proceedings or investigations pending or threatened against or affecting the Distributor's ability to fulfill its obligations under this Agreement, at law or in equity, or before any federal, state, county, municipal, or other governmental instrumentality or authority, domestic or foreign. Distributor warrants that all payments from subdistributors and other distributors will be by check, cash, wire transfer, letter of credit, or money order payable in the name of Distributor.

XI. INDEMNITY: Each party hereby agrees to defend, indemnify, and hold harmless the other (and its affiliates, and its and their respective successors, assigns, distributors, officers, directors, employees, subsidiaries, licensees, and representatives) against and for any and all claims, liabilities, damages, costs, and expenses (including reasonable outside attorney's fees and court costs) arising from or related to any breach or alleged breach (or claim which, if proven, would be such breach) by the indemnifying party of any of its undertakings, representations, or warranties under this Agreement, and/or arising from or related to any and all third-party claims which, if proven would be such breach. Each party agrees to notify the other in writing of any and all claims to which this indemnity will apply, and to afford the indemnifying party the opportunity to undertake the defense of such claim(s) with counsel approved by the indemnified party (which approval will not be unreasonably withheld), subject to the right of the indemnified party to participate in such defense at its cost. In no event shall any such claim be settled in such a way as would adversely affect the rights of the indemnified party in the Picture without such party's prior written consent; provided, however, that Producer hereby consents to any settlement entered into under any of the following circumstances:

A. the applicable insurance authorized the settlement;

B. the settlement relates to a claim for injunctive relief which has remained unsettled or pending for a period of thirty (30) days or longer which otherwise interferes with Distributor's distribution of the Picture hereunder; or the settlement is for not more than ten thousand dollars ($10,000). All rights and remedies of the parties hereunder will be cumulative and will not interfere with or prevent the exercise of any other right or remedy which may be available to the respective party.

XII. DELIVERY MATERIALS: The Picture will be delivered as follows: (a) Within fourteen (14) days of signing this document, Producer will deliver to Distributor the materials specified in Exhibit "A" hereto, accompanied by a fully executed lab access letter (irrevocable for the Term) for access to the Master materials, if applicable. If any said materials are not acceptable to Distributor, Distributor will notify the Producer of any technical problems or defects within ten (10) business days, and Producer will promptly replace the defective materials at Producer's sole expense. Distributor shall have no right to terminate this Agreement unless and until Producer has failed to cure any such defects within thirty (30) days after notice thereof from Distributor. If no objection is made within ten (10) business days of delivery of an item, the item will be deemed acceptable. If Distributor creates its own artwork and trailers for the Picture, ownership of these materials shall vest in Producer, and Producer shall have the right to use said materials after the Term of this Agreement expires. (b) Producer will concurrently with the delivery of the materials deliver to Distributor a list of contractual requirements for advertising credits to persons who rendered services or furnished materials for such Picture and a list of any restrictions. (c) All materials delivered to Distributor shall be returned to Producer within thirty (30) days of the end of the Term.

XIII. ADVANCE/GUARANTEE: There shall be no advance.

XIV. ALLOCATION OF GROSS RECEIPTS: As to proceeds derived from Distributor's exploitation of all rights outlined in Paragraph II, division of the Gross Receipts will be made as follows: (a) Gross Receipts: As used herein, the term "Gross Receipts" shall mean all monies actually received by and credited to Distributor, less any refunds, returns, credit card/bank fees, taxes, collection costs, shipping & handling, and manufacturing or duplication costs. Distributor may receive advances, guarantees, security deposits, and similar payments from persons or companies licensed by Distributor to subdistribute or otherwise exploit the Picture. Notwithstanding Distributor's receipt of such monies, if any, and not withstanding anything to the contrary contained herein, no such monies will be deemed to be Gross Receipts hereunder unless and until such monies are earned. (b) From the Distributor's exploitation of Home Video/DVD, Video On Demand, and Internet, Distributor shall recoup all Recoupable Expenses (see Paragraph XV). From the remaining revenues, Distributor shall deduct and retain thirty percent (30%) of Gross Receipts. The net proceeds shall be paid to Producer. Copies of all statements, notices, and reports shall be sent to Producer at the address set forth above. (c) Deductions from Gross Receipts shall be taken in the following order: (1) Recoupable Expenses incurred by Distributor, (2) Distribution Fee of thirty percent (30%) of Gross Receipts, (3) Net Proceeds shall be paid to Producer.

XV. RECOUPABLE EXPENSES: As used herein, the term "Expenses" and/or "Recoupable Expenses" shall mean all of Distributor's actual expenses on behalf of the Picture, limited as follows: (a) DVD production and replication costs: These expenses include all direct out-of-pocket costs to produce and replicate professional standard DVDs. (b) Internet costs include, but may not be limited to, transferring and encoding. (c) Promotional Expenses: These expenses include the cost of preparing artwork (e.g., DVD covers, Internet images), posters, one-sheet, trailers, and advertising relating to the Picture. (d) Delivery Expenses: Delivery Expenses are the direct out-of-pocket costs incurred by Distributor to manufacture any of the film, video, or digital deliverables (as listed on Exhibit "A") which Producer did not supply. Delivery Expenses also include the direct out-of-pocket costs incurred between markets for shipping, duplicating, and delivery of marketing materials (i.e., screeners) to foreign buyers, although Distributor will make best efforts to keep these low. At Producer's request, Distributor shall provide receipts for each and every expense. (e) Recoupable Expenses do not include any of the Distributor's general office overhead, but may include expenses tied directly to the management of Producer's materials (DVD inventory, fulfillment, communication).

XVI. DEFAULT/TERMINATION:
   A. Distributor Default: If it is found and proven that Distributor has defaulted on its obligations under this Agreement, upon notification in writing, including details of alleged default hereunder sufficient so as to enable Distributor to effectuate a cure, sent to the address above of that fact from Producer, Distributor will have thirty (30) days from receipt of said notice to cure said default. If the default is not cured within the allotted period, the Producer will have the right to initiate arbitration.
   B. Producer Default: Distributor shall notify Producer in writing, including details of alleged default hereunder sufficient so as to enable Producer to effectuate a cure. Producer shall have thirty (30) days from receipt of said notice to correct alleged default before Distributor initiates arbitration.
   C. Termination Rights: Failure by either party hereto to perform any of its obligations under this Agreement shall not be deemed to be a material breach of this Agreement until the nonbreaching party has given the breaching party written notice of its failure to perform, and such failure has not been corrected within ten (10) business days (thirty [30] days in the event of a monetary breach) from and after the giving of such notice. In the event of an incurred material breach, either party shall be entitled to terminate this Agreement (subject to arbitration) by written notice to the other party, obtain mon-

etary damages and other appropriate relief, and, in the case of Producer, regain all of its rights in the Picture from Distributor, provided that Producer shall continue to honor all existing executed contracts and licenses respecting Picture. Producer shall have the right to terminate this Agreement and cause all rights herein conveyed to Distributor to revert to Producer, provided that Producer shall continue to honor all third-party agreements conveying rights in the Picture (in respect to which Producer shall be deemed an assignee of all of Distributor's rights therein in respect to the Picture), by written notice to Distributor in the event that Distributor files a petition in bankruptcy or consents to an involuntary petition in bankruptcy or to any reorganization under Chapter 11 of the Bankruptcy Act or dissolved by action at law.

XVII. ACCOUNTINGS:

A. Distributor will render or cause to be rendered to Producer semiannual accounting statements showing expenses and receipts. Statements will be produced fifteen (15) days after the 30th of June and the 31st of December. Processing of these statements will begin six (6) months after the signing of this Agreement and delivery of materials listed in Exhibit "A." All monies due and payable to Producer pursuant to this Agreement will be paid simultaneously with the rendering of such statements. Distributor has the option to hold back up to five thousand dollars ($5,000) at the end of each six (6)-month window if funds are anticipated to be needed to cover Recoupable Expenses in the next six (6)-month window.

B. Producer will be deemed to have consented to all accountings rendered by Distributor or its assignees or successors, and all such statements will be binding upon Producer unless specific objections in writing, stating the basis thereof, are given within ten (10) days after receipt of statements by Producer.

C. Distributor shall keep and maintain at its office, until expiration of the Term and for a period of three (3) years thereafter, complete detailed, permanent, true, and accurate books of account and records relating to the distributing and exhibition of the Picture, including, but not limited to, detailed collections and sales by country and/or buyer, detailed billings thereon, detailed play dates if applicable thereof, detailed records of expenses that have been deducted from collections received from the exploitation of the Picture, and the whereabouts of prints, trailers, accessories, and other material in connection with the Picture. Records shall be kept in accordance with Generally Accepted Accounting Principles (GAAP). Producer shall be entitled to inspect such books and records of Distributor relating to the Picture during regular business hours, and shall be entitled to audit such books and records of Distributor relating to the Picture upon ten (10) business days' written notice to Distributor, and provided that not more than one audit is conducted every twelve (12) months during each calendar year, and further provided that such audit shall last not more than ten (10) consecutive business days once begun and does not interfere with Distributor's normal operations. Within thirty (30) days of the completion of the audit, Producer will furnish Distributor with a copy of said audit. In the event that the audit discloses that Producer has been underpaid twenty-five thousand dollars ($25,000) or more, Distributor shall reimburse Producer for all reasonable •• be borne by Producer.

XVIII. NOTICES: All notices and other communications under this Agreement will be in writing and will be deemed given when delivered by hand or upon confirmed receipt of a facsimile transmission, two (2) days after being deposited with an overnight courier, or five (5) days after mailing, postage prepaid, by registered or certified mail, return receipt requested, to the address and numbers specified above or such other addresses as either party will specify in a written notice to the other. In all instances, hard copies will follow all fax correspondence.

XIX. ASSIGNMENT: This Agreement will be binding upon and will inure to the benefit of the parties hereto and their respective successors and permitted assigns. Producer may assign its rights to payment of monies. Distributor may assign its rights without the prior written consent of Producer, provided that Distributor assigns its rights to a successor company that may arise from Distributor's merging, being acquired, or partnering with another company.

XX. DISPUTE RESOLUTION: The parties agree that, in the event of an alleged breach or a dispute ("Dispute") in connection with this Agreement, they will first work together in good faith to resolve the matter informally by discussions between their management. In the event such attempts have not resolved the Dispute within forty-five (45) days following either party's request to resolve a Dispute, the Dispute will be settled by binding confidential arbitration administered by the American Arbitration Association ("AAA") in accordance with its then-applicable rules. The arbitration will be conducted in San Francisco, California, U.S.A., in English, by a single arbitrator familiar with entertainment law, who will be selected by mutual agreement of the parties, or, if the parties cannot agree, by the AAA. The award of the arbitrator will be final and binding, and judgment on the award may be entered and enforced in any court having jurisdiction thereof. The parties agree to equally share the fees and expenses of the arbitrator. For purposes of the Convention on the Recognition and Enforcement of Foreign Arbitral Awards of 1958, known as the "New York Convention," the award will be deemed an award of the United States. Nothing in this section will preclude either party from seeking interim or provisional relief concerning any breach or dispute, including a temporary restraining order, a preliminary injunction, or an order of attachment, either prior to or during informal discussions or arbitration.

XXI. ENTIRE AGREEMENT: This Agreement is intended by the parties hereto as a final expression of their Agreement and understanding with respect to the subject matter hereof, and as a complete and exclusive statement of the terms thereof (unless amended in writing by both parties), and supersedes any and all prior and contemporaneous agreements and understanding thereto. This Agreement will be understood to in all respects lay under the jurisdiction of California law and the laws of the United States of America. In the event of any conflict or action between the parties, the prevailing party shall be entitled to recoup its reasonable attorney fees and court costs and expenses from the nonprevailing party. Paragraph headings in this Agreement are used for convenience only, and will not be used to interpret or construe the provisions of this Agreement.

IN WITNESS WHEREOF, the parties have executed this Agreement as of the date hereof.

AGREED AND ACCEPTED: FILM COMPANY:

By: _____   Date: _____

By: _____   Date: _____

Appendix C

Twelve Ways to Market Your Film for Self-Distribution

One of the biggest questions I get asked by filmmakers who are interested in to pursuing self-distribution is how they can spread the word in order to drive sales of their movie, whether it is ticket sales, DVD sales, or downloads.

In my mind, one of the most important things to consider when developing your marketing strategy is to define who your core audience is. The major studios hyper-analyze a movie's core audience before they decide to go into a production with it, so for independents considering self-distribution, analyzing your core audience is a must. Once you define who your target group is, you can develop your marketing strategy from there.

Remember, the anchor of your marketing strategy should always be your film's website or blog because this is where people can go to get additional info or buy your products.

Here are twelve effective ways to market your film for self-distribution, whether you have a budget or not.

1. **Post Your Trailer Online**
   I gave some examples of where to post your trailer online in the book, but what I didn't mention is that by posting your trailer online, it is actually a great way to spread the word for your film. Posting your trailer online gives you a shot at harnessing the power of viral video, the possibility that your trailer

will be spread around the internet, and access to hundreds or thousands of people who will link back to your website where they can purchase your DVD, pay for a download, or learn about a theatrical screening in their town.

2. **Hire A Publicist**

   As I mentioned before, publicists are worth their weight in gold and one of the easiest and most effective ways to market your film to the masses is to hire a professional publicist to get you press. They can work on both national press (like magazines, television, and radio), as well as local press if, for example, you are releasing your film in specific markets.

3. **Buy Advertising**

   Advertising is an instant way to grab the attention of your potential audience and get them to your website. You can go the route of buying small ads in trade magazines or newsletters, as well as getting in the Internet advertising game. Go to specific websites where you think your potential audience frequents (example: gaming websites can be a great way to reach a young male audience), and look into buying a small ad there. The great thing about buying advertising is you can start small, and then if it works, you can roll it out bigger. And you can link people directly to your site where they can purchase a copy of your film.

4. **Post On Message Boards**

   If you trying to market your film on little or no budget, posting on relevant message boards is a great way to spread the word on the cheap. Simply go to community-oriented websites that are related to your core audience (i.e.: are you trying to market to a Christian audience? A teen audience? A Hispanic audience?) and participate in the message boards while inserting the link to your film's website in your signature. If you are going this route, it is important to keep in mind that you should actually contribute valuable advice and opinions on the message boards before starting to heavily promote your film. First gain the trust of the community, and then introduce them to your film. You are much more likely to have actual buyers that way!

5. **Contact Local Radio**

   People tend to overlook radio as a significant source of PR, but it is actually a great way to reach a core audience. Flip through your radio dial and check out all the talk networks that do interviews with local artists, entrepreneurs, and business people. Call them up and tell them you want to submit a press release for your movie and request an interview, but make sure you give them a good reason to want to interview you (such as you just finished shooting your film locally, or some other similar hook). You can also do all this through the radio station's website. If they agree to interview you, you'll gain an incredible reach of an audience and you can link people back to your website to hopefully purchase a copy of your film.

6. **Contact Local Newspapers**

   Like radio, don't discount the power of local newspapers either! The easiest way to get an interview in local newspapers is to pick up a copy (or look at a copy online), look at the list of editors usually on the first page, and contact them directly to offer up an interview. Again, you'll need some kind of hook as to why they would interview you (like you shot your film in the local café, or you're getting ready to do your theatrical premiere in a week). However, in my experience, local papers are always on the lookout for new stories and believe it or not, people read those things!

7. **Get Interviewed For A Pod Cast**

   There are so many pod casts out there now and they are gaining bigger and bigger audiences every day. Start with iTunes or Podcast Alley (www.podcastalley.com) and do a search for pod casts that are related to your core audience. Otherwise, search for indie film podcasts (there are many!) and contact the hosts and tell them about a creative way you utilized to shoot your film, a new camera you used, or a particular tool you used in post, and offer to be interviewed about it. I've gotten several pod cast interviews myself by contacting the hosts directly, so I know this works. And it is a great way to direct traffic to your site where you are selling your DVD's!

8. **Do Your Own Podcast**

   If you are unable to find a podcast that you want to contribute to, then create your own and get it listed on iTunes and other podcast directories like Podcast Alley. These days, all you need is a simple microphone attached to your computer to record a pod cast, and then convert it to QuickTime to upload to the web. I know several filmmakers who created a series of pod-casts for their films, and soon they gained an audience and momentum and it helped tremendously with sales of their DVD's. They also were able to launch platform theatrical releases off the back of successful podcast series since you only need to take a survey of where most of your listeners are, and then look into releasing your film in those markets.

9. **Enter Film Festivals**

   It may seem obvious, but entering your film in film festivals can also help spread the word for your film. Heck, you can even sell copies of your DVD's right there at screenings, which is a perfect time to catch people (right after they've enjoyed watching your film hopefully!). The other great thing about film festivals is that you have the opportunity to gain some local press, especially if you win any type of award, and in that press you can include the link to your website where your DVD's are for sale. If your film creates a serious buzz at a festival, you can always return to the city where the festival is and put your film in the local theater for a week and see how it does. In other words, you can leverage the buzz your film got at the festival and turn it into a theatrical release.

10. **Email Campaigns**

   Another obvious way to promote your self-distributed film is to do some email marketing campaigns. Start with everyone you know and send out a couple promotion emails with links to your website where people can view the trailer and purchase your DVD. Ask people in the email to forward the email on to anyone they know who might be interested in your film, and start to build word of mouth that way. Another way to harness the power of email is to ask related websites if they will send an email out to their community on your behalf with a little review of your film and a link to your site. Trust me; if you have a film that appeals to a core audience, (anything from skateboarders and gore seekers to Alaskans) related Web sites' communities would want to know about your film!

11. **Have House Parties Or Local Screenings**

House parties and local screenings at churches and schools can be a form of self-distribution in its own right, as well as serve as a great marketing tool for selling your DVD's and building a buzz for your film before putting it in theaters. The way to set up house parties and local screenings is by picking a date and place, emailing invites to everyone you know, posting fliers around, and collaborating with the venues for cross-promotional opportunities (ex: maybe the church can put an announcement in their weekly bulletin, etc.).

12. **Make Fliers and Posters**

Another obvious solution for marketing your indie film is good old- fashioned fliers and posters. Print them up yourself or get them done professionally, but make sure they don't look ama- teurish. Remember, you're trying to sell a product here! You can place the posters and fliers in local theaters where you will be screening in order to promote your film in advance, and get people to show up and buy tickets. You can also place them in local cafes, bookstores, and anywhere else they might be picked up by a potential buyer or customer. Be sure to list the screen- ing locations and times as well as your Web address for addi- tional info. Spend time studying what other professionally done film posters and fliers look like and stick to the format that works. For example, if you go into your local video store you will see posters of movies that studios are promoting . . . just copy that format and then see if the video store will hang your poster in there and agree to sell your video!

Appendix D

More Sample Contracts

Subject to Contract

A. <u>Date</u>
B. <u>Parties</u> (i) Name of Company A/ Licensor Address
("Licensor" which expression shall include Permitted Transferees)
     (ii) Name of Company B Address
("Company B" which expression shall include Permitted Transferees)
C. <u>Definitions</u> As set forth in clauses A–J hereof and in clause 1 of the general conditions (the "Conditions") annexed hereto.
D. <u>Licence</u> Licensor hereby grants to Company B by way of exclusive licence under copyright the Rights in and to the Programme in the Territory on and subject to the terms set forth herein and in the Conditions.
E. <u>The Programme</u> herein licensed by Licensor and the licence fee for the Programme (the "Licence Fee") are as follows:

Title	Licence Fee
"Name of Programme"	£3,000

F. The Licence Fee in respect of the Programme shall be payable as follows:

Event	Amount
Upon Delivery Date	50% of the Licence Fee
On 1st November 2006	50% of the Licence Fee

G. Definitions
   (a) "Availability Date": in respect of the Programme: 1ˢᵗ September 2006
   (b) "Licence Period": in respect of the Programme: a period commencing on the Availability Date and continuing for three (3) years after the later of the Availability Date or the Delivery Date.
   (c) "NVOD": means the exhibition of programming by any means of Television where an individual exhibition fee charge on a per-exhibition basis is made by a viewer for the privilege of viewing that particular programme or film and where such programme or film is scheduled by the broadcaster at frequent intervals of less than fifteen (15) minutes apart.

H. Number of Exhibitions:
   Maximum Number of Exhibition Weeks in respect of the Programme on any Primary Channel and multiplex versions thereof as provided in clause 1.8 of the Conditions: unlimited

I. Special Conditions
   (a) All Materials as specified in clause 3.1 of the Conditions shall be delivered, by courier, to:
   Name of Contact at Company B Address
   (b) Company B shall pay the relevant Licence Fee(s) due pursuant to this Agreement by the relevant Payment Date. "Payment Date" means the date(s) set out in Clause F above save that no Licence Fee shall be payable until 45 days after receipt by Company B of an appropriate invoice. Invoices should be addressed for the attention of "Name of contact at Company B" the address set out in clause I(a) above.
   (c) If payment has not been made by the Payment Date, Licensor may charge interest on any outstanding uncontested sums, at the rate of 2% above the base rate from time to time of "Name of Bank" from the relevant Payment Date until payment by Company B of the relevant uncontested sum due hereunder. Such interest shall accrue and be calculated on a daily basis.

(d) Company B shall be entitled to exhibit the Programme on any channel, including, for the avoidance of doubt and without limitation, any multiplex versions of any channel, broadcast by Company B or any Subsidiary or Associated Company during the Licence Period.

(e) For the purposes of clause 1.8 and clause 2 of the Conditions only, the words "including without limitation the "Internet" in lines 5 and 6 of clause 1.11 of the Conditions shall be deemed to have been deleted and replaced by the words "excluding the "Internet". Further, also for the purposes of clause 1.8 and clause 2 of the Conditions only, the definition of Television in clause 1.11 of the Conditions shall be deemed to exclude Pay-Per-View, Video-On-Demand, SVOD, NVOD and delivery via mobile telecommunication systems.

(f) Clause 1.8.4 of the Conditions shall be deemed deleted.

(g) For the avoidance of doubt, the Licence Fee shall include any and all costs and expenses incurred in relation to the creation of any Masters in respect of the Programme to be supplied in accordance with this Agreement.

(h) Notwithstanding anything to the contrary in this Agreement, Company B shall be responsible for any Broadcast Grand Rights Payments (defined below) due in connection with Company B's broadcast of the Programme(s) during the Licence Period PROVIDED THAT the Licensor has notified Company B in writing no later than one (1) month prior to the Availability Date that such Payments are required.

For the purposes of this Agreement, broadcast grand rights payments ("**Broadcast Grand Rights Payments**") shall mean payments payable to the relevant copyright owner and that generally arise in connection with the broadcast of dramatic presentations (of the complete work or extracts) of copyright operas, operettas, stage (not film) musicals and ballets.

Company B's responsibility herein shall be limited to payment of Broadcast Grand Rights Payments and it is the sole responsibility of the Licensor to clear and/or pay for any and all grand right synchronisation fees (as such terms are currently understood in the film and music industry in the Territory as at the date hereof) that arise in connection with the recording of the Programme(s).

If the Licensor fails to notify Company B of any Broadcast Grand Rights Payments that will arise out of or in connection with Company B's broadcast of the Programme(s), the Licensor agrees, warrants and represents that Licensor has either fully cleared any and all Broadcast Grand Rights Payments or that no Broadcast Grand Rights Payments will arise out of or in connection with Company B's broadcast of the Programme(s) during the Licence Period.

In the event that Company B is obliged to make any Broadcast Grand Rights Payments in connection with its broadcast of the Programme(s) and the Licensor has failed to notify Company B in accordance with this Special Condition clause I (h) that such Payments will arise out of or in connection with such broadcast (**"Additional Payments"**), Company B shall provide to the Licensor a document certifying the Additional Payments made and the Licensor shall immediately repay to Company B such Additional Payments. Alternatively, Company B shall be entitled to set off such Additional Payments against any payments owing to the Licensor including, without limitation, Licence Fees due to it under the terms of this Agreement.

In the event that the Licensor notifies Company B less than one (1) month prior to the Availability Date that Broadcast Grand Rights Payments will arise out of or in connection with Company B's broadcast of the Programme(s) or if any Additional Payments are not repaid to Company B within forty-five (45) days of Company B providing the appropriate documentation to the Licensor, Company B shall have the right at its sole discretion to terminate this Agreement and Licensor shall forthwith repay to Company B such amount reduced on a pro rata basis based on the number of Exhibition Days that the Programme was exhibited by Company B subject to the above right to set off with respect to Additional Payments for such Exhibition Days. Company B's right to terminate shall be without prejudice to Company B's other rights or remedies against the Licensor hereunder.

(i)   The words "at least one hundred and fifty (150) days" in line 2 of clause 3.1 of the Conditions shall be deemed deleted and replaced by the words "no later than six (6) weeks".

(j)   The Licensor acknowledges that it will be solely responsible for the costs of delivery of the Materials set out in clause 3.1 of the Conditions.

(k)   The Licensor shall grant Company B access to any relevant website for the purposes of downloading publicity and promotional materials in respect of the Programme.

(l)   Company B acknowledges that it may not use or authorise the use of the name and/or likeness of NAME OF ARTIST, NAME OF ARTIST, and/or NAME OF ARTIST in its promotion(s) of its exhibition of the Programme. Further, Company B acknowledges that it may not use any songs or soundtracks other than those of the Licensor in the creation of trailers or other promotional videos for the Programme without the prior written consent of the Licensor.

(m) In the event the first Master delivered by the Licensor has been accepted by Company B in accordance with the terms of this Agreement, the word "Licensor's" in line 5 of clause 3.3 of the Conditions shall be deemed deleted and replaced with the word "Company B's".

(n)   Clause 7 of the Conditions shall be deemed deleted and replaced with the following clause 7:
"Each party shall be responsible for its own tax liabilities in their respective Territory, including any company or corporate tax, national taxes, federal or state taxes, and all such payments hereunder shall be made without any deduction other than withholding (if applicable). In the event that either party is obliged to make a payment for

withholding tax, then the party who is responsible shall pay the amount withheld promptly to the appropriate authority and shall provide the other party with a verified original document (or other reasonable evidence) certifying that the amounts withheld has or will be accounted for to the appropriate authority."

(o) Both Company B and the Licensor acknowledge that Company B's first exhibition on Television of the Programme shall be a Television premiere in the Territory and Company B shall be entitled to refer to it as such.

(p) Company B shall have the option to relicense the Programme on terms to be negotiated in good faith, such option to be exercised by Company B no later than 31st May 2009.

J. Agreement

This agreement shall consist of clauses A–J hereof together with the Conditions and Attachment A which are hereby incorporated. In the event of any inconsistency between the Conditions, Attachment A and clauses A–J hereof, clauses A–J shall prevail.

AS WITNESS the hands of the authorised signatories on behalf of the parties the day and year first above written.

SIGNED by

_____

for and on behalf of
Company A, Inc.

SIGNED by

_____

for and on behalf of
Company B

Company B

Programme Purchase Agreement
General Conditions

1. <u>Definitions</u>

For the purposes of the agreement consisting of clauses A–J inclusive and these Conditions (hereinafter "the Agreement") the following words shall have the meanings hereby ascribed to them and words and phrases defined in clauses A–J inclusive of the Agreement shall have the same meanings in these Conditions:

1.1. "Associated Company" shall have the meaning attributed to it in Section 416 of the Income and Corporation Taxes Act 1988 save that references to "company" and cognate expressions shall be deemed to include references to "body corporate".

1.2. "Delivery Date" in respect of each Programme, means the date on which the materials listed in clause 3.1 are delivered to Company B provided always that delivery shall not be deemed to have taken place until such time as an acceptable Master shall have been delivered and accepted by Company B in accordance with clause 3.2.

1.3. "Exhibition Week" means a seven day period commencing from the time of first transmission of each Programme during which period each Programme may be exhibited up to three (3) times.

1.4. "Master" means as requested by Company B one high definition HD 1080/25/I and/or standard definition pure 625 component Digital Betacam in accordance with the technical specifications set out in Attachment A and being a direct digital dub sourced directly from a 35 mm Programme with stereo sound. Such Masters shall be provided as follows:

    1.4.1. Language: supplied in English or in original language with English sub-titles.

    1.4.2. Format: a 16:9 full height anamorphically compressed Pal Digital Betacam. If a 16:9 fullheight version is not available, then subject to Company B's prior written consent, Licensor may offer to supply a 16:9 letterbox 1:75/1:85/2:35 version. If the foregoing version is not available, then subject to Company B's prior written consent, Licensor may offer to supply a 4:3 fullheight version.

1.4.3. All Masters shall be supplied in colour (unless originated in black and white) with stereo audio. Mono versions of stereo recordings are not acceptable.

1.4.4. The technical specifications for Master(s) set out in Attachment A are subject to change from time to time by Company B providing reasonable written notice to Licensor. Company B's decision as to whether or not to accept materials other than in the PAL Digital Betacam format as specified above is in its sole discretion.

1.5. "Pay-Per-View" and/or "Video-On-Demand" ("PPV" and/or "VOD") mean the exhibition of programming by any means of Television where an individual exhibition fee is charged on a per-exhibition basis for the privilege of viewing that particular programme or Programme.

1.6. "Performances" shall include acting, mime, dance, speech, production, direction, singing and playing an instrument or conducting (whether alone or with others).

1.7. "the Programme(s)" means the Programme(s) details of which are specified in clause E of the Agreement.

1.8. "Rights" means in respect of each of the Programmes the following rights granted by Licensor to Company B hereunder all of which shall be exclusive and may be exercised throughout the Term unless otherwise indicated namely:

1.8.1. The right to exhibit from any place and/or authorise others to exhibit from any place the

Programme(s) during the Licence Period(s) by means of Television in the Territory. Company B shall be entitled to exercise the Rights hereunder on any channel broadcast by Company B or any Subsidiary or Associated Company.

1.8.2. The right to exhibit the Programmes on up to four (4) multiplexed versions of any main channel on which such Programme is exhibited (such main channel is hereafter the "Primary Channel") e.g. up to four (4) versions of the Primary Channel (in addition to the Primary Channel) on which the programming is similar to or similarly branded to the Primary Channel.

1.8.3. The right to exhibit each Programme for up to the Maximum Number of Exhibition Weeks on each channel on which such Programme is exhibited. For the avoidance of doubt:

a) a simultaneous retransmission by third parties of Company B's signal of the channels on which any such Programme is exhibited shall count only as the same one (1) exhibition; and

b) the exhibition rights granted hereunder shall apply separately and additionally to the exhibition of a Programme on each and every channel on which such Programme is exhibited. (For the purposes of what constitutes an exhibition rights hereunder apply and are granted in respect of each Programme separately and additionally to exhibition on any satellite/cable channel, any DTT delivered channel and any multiplexed version of a Primary Channel).

1.8.4. The right to exhibit from any place and/or authorise others to exhibit from any place the Programme(s) during the Licence Period(s) on SVOD in the Territory. Company B shall be entitled to exercise the Rights hereunder on any SVOD service provided by Company or any Subsidiary or Associated Company.

1.8.5.   The right to exhibit to any place and/or authorise others to exhibit to any place the Programme(s) during the Licence Period(s) by means of Television in the Territory whether on a pay and/or free basis.

1.8.6.   The right to make Company B's Sub-Masters.

1.8.7.   The right to cut and/or edit the Programme for the purposes of meeting censorship requirements and/or relevant guidelines and/or programming timing needs as required by Company B's service, at Company B's own discretion and cost.

1.8.8.   The right, where Company B, in its sole discretion, deems it appropriate, to reversion and to retitle onto Company B's Sub Masters only.

1.8.9.   The right, without prejudice to any other Rights and remedies under this Agreement, to insert reasonable statements about transmission quality (by means of illustration only, to alert viewers about strobe-effects).

1.8.10. The right, without prejudice to any other Rights and remedies under this Agreement when Company B believes, in its sole reasonable opinion that the exhibition of the Programme may (a) be defamatory or contrary to law; or (b) infringe the copyright, performing right, right of privacy trademark or other proprietary right of any third party; or (c) cause Company B to be in breach of any law, regulation or Code of Practice or the provisions of any other agreement then Company B may omit the whole, but not part of such Programme and shall inform Licensor forthwith. In the event that Company B omits the Programme pursuant to this sub-clause, then

Licensor shall reimburse Company B for Licence Fees attributable to such Programme.

1.8.11. The right to Subtitle, exhibit and authorise others to exhibit Subtitled versions of the Programme(s)/Programme(s). "Subtitle" shall mean the inclusion of text, signing, and/or audio description.

1.8.12. The right to insert and interpolate advertisements and sponsorship billboards at appropriate intervals in the Programme and to include the Programme (during the Licence Period) in any sponsored season or slot.

1.8.13. The right, prior to and during the Term, in connection with the advertising, publicising and promotion of Company B's services:

a) to reproduce and transmit and authorise others to reproduce and transmit excerpts from the Programme (not to exceed three (3) minutes per excerpt) on any of Company B's services or on the services of third parties or otherwise in any part of the Territory;

b) to reproduce and publish still photographs and/or brief synopses of the Programme and the right to authorise others to do the same;

c) authorise others to transmit excerpted and/or 'grabbed' still images or moving clips with or without the accompanying soundtrack and/or audio material from the Programme in local and wide area computer networks (e.g. the Internet) notwithstanding the fact that such computer networks extend beyond the geographical limits of the Territory and such material may be capable of receipt anywhere on such networks; and

d) to transmit and authorise others to transmit excerpted still images or moving clips with or without the accompanying soundtrack and or audio material from the Programme as part of the electronic programme guides ("EPGs").

1.8.14. The right to reproduce, transmit and authorise others to reproduce and transmit excerpted and or "grabbed" still images of moving clips (not to exceed three (3) minutes per excerpt) on any of Company B's television services with or without the accompanying soundtrack and/or audio material from the Programme for interstitial purposes, subject to section I-L above.

1.8.15. Subject to section I-L above, the right to use and publish in respect of the artists, producers, directors, musicians and other performers whose Performances are covered or reproduced in the Programme(s) or any other person concerned in the making thereof, their legal or professional names, photographs and likenesses in connection with the promotion and advertising of Company B's services provided always that Company B shall comply with all credit requirements notified in writing to Company B by Licensor prior to delivery of the Master of such Programme. Company B shall not be liable for any casual or inadvertent failure to comply with the provisions of this sub-clause.

1.8.16. The right to broadcast or authorise others to broadcast the Programme simultaneously on two (2) or more satellites and such simultaneous transmission shall constitute the same one (1) exhibition.

1.8.17. The right to make and retain both during and after the Term a copy of any Programme as may be required or recommended by any relevant authority.

1.8.18. The right to include icons on the Programmes that may enable such viewer in the course of viewing exhibitions of the Programme(s) to access on demand and/or select from a range of options enhanced service(s) available through Company B's interactive platform or any part thereof including without limitation, navigational tools such as EPG functionality and other applications such as digital text and screen shrinkage and other forms of enhancements hereafter developed from time to time.

1.8.19. In respect of programmes which are concerts or recital performances containing a variety of musical works and subject to the provisions of this clause, Company B reserves the right to transmit such programmes in two parts on successive days or in successive weeks, such a split transmission being counted as one run or playday for the programme when both parts have been transmitted. Programmes presented under the provisions of this clause shall be presented, billed and listed as Part One and Part Two of the programme under its normal title and shall not be otherwise altered or edited. Notwithstanding the forgoing, Company B undertakes that it shall not transmit such a programme in two or more parts when in respect of that programme Licensor has given notice that the producer has prohibited any such non-continuous transmission of the programme.

1.9. "SVOD" shall mean a subscription or "value added" service, transmitted by any means of delivery, which offers the viewer access to programmes or a block of programming for the selection and exhibition of individual programmes at a time determined by the viewer. Notwithstanding anything to the contrary in this Agreement and without limitation, the Internet (and other analogous open user networks) and PVR downloads shall be deemed to be included in the scope of the means of delivery for which Rights for SVOD are granted.

1.10. "Subsidiary" shall have the meaning attributed to it by Section 736 of the Companies Act 1985 (as amended by Section 144 of the Companies Act 1989) but (for the avoidance of doubt) as if all references therein to companies included any body corporate, wherever incorporated.

1.11. "Television" means all forms of communication to the public by way of electronic transmission now known or hereafter developed whether analogue and/or digital or otherwise of audio and/or audio visual and/or video signals now known or hereafter developed including without limitation delivery via one or more of the following: satellite; cable; SMATV; microwave; MMDS; DTT.

1.12. The "Term" means the period commencing on the earlier of the date hereof or sixty (60) days prior to the Availability Date for the first Programme hereunder continuing until the last day of the Licence Period for the Programme last to expire hereunder.

1.13. "Territory" means United Kingdom of Great Britain and Northern Ireland, Republic of Ireland, Channel Islands and Isle of Man.

1.14. "Company B's Sub-Master" means such copy or copies of the Master loaned to Company B hereunder as Company B shall manufacture or cause to be manufactured for the purpose of exercising the Rights hereunder (but not further or otherwise).

2. Licensor Holdbacks

   2.1. Licensor confirms and undertakes with respect to each Programme that prior to the Licence Period no version of such Programme will have been promoted or exhibited in the Territory on Television by any means including without limitation pay and free Television and transactional services such as PPV, VOD and SVOD.

   2.2. Licensor confirms and undertakes with respect to each Programme that Licensor shall not at any time during the Licence Period directly or indirectly exhibit or promote the exhibitions of any versions of such Programme in the Territory by any form of Television by any means including without limitation pay and free Television and transactional services such as PPV, VOD and SVOD.

2.3. Licensor confirms and undertakes with respect to each Programme that Licensor has not directly or indirectly authorised prior to the Term and shall not authorise any third party to exhibit or promote the exhibitions at any time during the Licence Period of any versions of such Programme in the Territory by any form of Television by any means including without limitation pay and free Television and transactional services such as PPV, VOD and SVOD.

2.4. With respect to each Programme, in the event of any breach of clauses 2.1, 2.2 or 2.3 and without prejudice to any of Company B's rights (including, without limitation to restrain, or to require Licensor to restrain, any further breaches of the said clauses) Company B may terminate the Agreement with respect to such Programme as provided in clause 8 below.

3. Materials

3.1. Licensor shall deliver to Company B at Licensor's sole cost and expense at least one hundred and fifty (150) days prior to the Availability Date in respect of each of the Programmes licensed hereunder the following materials and in respect of each Programme failure to comply with the provisions of this sub-clause shall be a material breach:

3.1.1. One Master on loan, such Master to be of a first class technical quality suitable for the manufacture by Company B of Company B's Sub-Masters if required or, if not required, suitable for transmission authorised under this Agreement.

3.1.2. One copy of the music cue sheet.

3.1.3. The following advertising or promotional materials:
a) a synopsis and cast list (with full biographical details) for the Programme;

b) if the Programme is a feature film, one United Kingdom theatrical trailer for the Programme, if available;

c) one electronic press kit for the Programme, if available;

d) colour transparencies of the Programme as available from stock e-mailed to Company B in jpeg format convertible by Company B;

e) in addition to the materials specified in sub-clauses (a) to (d) inclusive above, such additional trailer elements and advertising and promotional material (including photographs and biographies of artists and performers engaged in connection with the production of such Programme) general synopsis, episode synopses, full cast list and credits, transparencies and stills and any Programme trailers and copies of such other advertising and promotional materials as Company B may reasonably require in sufficient quantities and of sufficient quality as shall in the opinion of Company B enable Company B to promote and advertise such Programme and/or Company B's services generally; and

f) if requested, a time coded script to assist with reversioning. This script shall be supplied via e-mail as a word processing package that is convertible by Company B.

3.1.4.   A copy of the caption file via e-mail. Such file shall be PAL EBU caption files in the standard Teletext SoftelΣTL file format. If that is not available, then one copy of the dialogue and continuity script by prior written agreement. This script shall be supplied via e-mail as a word processing package that is convertible by Company B.

3.2.   Within forty five (45) days of receipt of a Master, Company B shall view the same to determine its technical acceptability PROVIDED ALWAYS that in the event that five (5) or more Masters are supplied pursuant to this Agreement in any forty five (45) day period then Company B shall be entitled to an additional period of twenty (20) days for each additional Master over four (4) so supplied in which to determine its technical acceptability. If Company B regards the Master as unacceptable it shall serve a notice rejecting the same within such forty five (45) days (or such additional period, if applicable) and shall promptly send a technical report to Licensor and further, if so requested by Licensor, shall promptly return the Master with such technical report to Licensor at Licensor's sole cost and expense. Licensor shall forthwith upon receipt of such notice but in no circumstances more than thirty (30) days after receipt of such notice dispatch at its sole cost and expense an alternative Master and the same procedure shall be repeated. If this second Master should be of unacceptable quality to Company B, Company B shall be entitled to terminate this Agreement by written notice in respect of the Programme contained on the said Master whereupon Licensor shall repay to Company B forthwith all sums paid by Company B to Licensor in respect of such Programme PROVIDED ALWAYS that if the unacceptable Master is part of a series the continuity of which would be seriously impaired by the inability to show the episode(s) contained on the unacceptable Master then Company B shall so notify Licensor and this Agreement shall forthwith terminate in respect of all the of the Programmes in such series and Licensor shall repay to Company B forthwith all sums paid by Company B in respect of such Programmes. Thereafter neither party shall have any further liability to the other in respect of such Programme.

3.3.   Company B shall be entitled to manufacture and retain Company B's Sub-Masters during the Term and to utilise the same for the transmission of its service. Following manufacture of Company B's Sub-Masters the Master shall be returned to Licensor in the same condition (fair wear and tear excepted) as that in which it was delivered at such address as Licensor shall nominate or direct. This delivery shall be at Licensor's sole cost and expense.

3.4.   In respect of any feature film that is licensed hereunder (if any) the version of each to be delivered hereunder shall be the version certificated by the British Board of Programme Classification or any successor body ("the BBFC") for home video.

3.5.   In respect of any feature film that is licensed hereunder (if any) Company B shall not be required to accept any film hereunder unless the BBFC has awarded such film an 18 or less restrictive certification in respect of both theatrical and home video exhibition or, where there is no theatrical exhibition, in respect of home video exhibition only.

3.6.   In respect of any feature film that is licensed hereunder (if any) Licensor shall provide to Company B no later than the Delivery Date a copy of the BBFC certificate and a copy of the UK Video Censor's Cut List if such list exists.

3.7.   In respect of any feature film that is licensed hereunder (if any) Licensor shall if so requested by Company B supply to Company B at Licensor's sole cost and expense a Master of the "airline version" or the "television version" (as such terms are commonly understood in the Programme industry in the Territory as at the date hereof) (if available) no later than 14 days after such request from Company B.

4. Licensor Representations, Warranties and Covenants
    Licensor represents and warrants that:

4.1.   It is the owner of the Rights in the Programmes which are granted to Company B hereunder and that the consent in writing of all performers has been secured whose Performances are reproduced in the Programmes and all other consents necessary for the elective grant to and exercise by Company B of the Rights in accordance with the terms of this Agreement.

4.2.   Company B shall be under no liability whatsoever to any of the said performers or any producers, directors or to any other third party rendering services in connection with the production and/or distribution and exploitation of the Programmes, the trailer elements, and advertising and promotional material (or to any person or body representing them) arising out of the exercise by Company B of the Rights (including by way of illustration and not limitation the payment of any and all royalties, participations, re-use fees, residual fees, re-run fees or other payments of whatsoever nature to any or all of the persons aforesaid or to any guilds or unions representing such persons for the privilege or right of exploiting or marketing the Programmes pursuant to the Rights granted to Company B hereunder).

4.3.   It possesses full power and authority to enter into and perform this Agreement and that there are no liens or encumbrances against the Programmes or any of them which would or might derogate from or be inconsistent with the Rights granted to Company B hereunder.

4.4.   The Programmes do not and will not contain material which is obscene or defamatory or which will or might expose Company B to any proceedings whatsoever of a civil nature from third parties (including but not limited to proceedings in respect of invasion of or breach of rights of privacy) or to criminal proceedings. Further the Programmes do and will comply in all respects with all relevant legislation, codes of practice or other regulations to which Company B is or may be from time to time subject, including but not limited to the codes of XXX (or any successor).

4.5.   Subject to the proviso to this sub-clause it is solely responsible for the fulfilment of all copyright and contractual obligations to third parties arising out of or in connection

with any musical, literary or dramatic work and/or
Performances reproduced in the Programmes and the
exploitation thereof pursuant to the Rights granted hereunder PROVIDED THAT Licensor shall not be responsible for securing those necessary music performance
rights in connection with such exploitation as aforesaid
as are vested in the appropriate collecting society.

4.6.   The Programmes are protected by copyright in the Territory and it will not do, procure or permit any act or
omission which would adversely affect such copyright
protection in any way whatsoever.

4.7.   Licensor will at the request of Company B and at Licensor's sole expense do all such further acts and execute
all such further deeds, documents and instruments from
time to time reasonably necessary to vest the Rights in
Company B and for the protection and enforcement of
the same and Licensor hereby appoints Company B its
agent with the right but not the obligation (at the sole
expense of Licensor) to do any and all acts and things
necessary to vest the Rights in Company B and to execute
all such further deeds, documents and instruments in
the name of and on behalf of Licensor which appointment shall be irrevocable. Company B's appointment as
agent is without prejudice to Company B's rights and
remedies with respect to breach of the above and without
detracting from Licensor's obligations.

4.8.   Licensor hereby undertakes prior to the commencement
of the Licence Period of each of the Programmes, at its
own cost, to effect with an established insurer and maintain until the end of the Term Errors and Omissions
insurance upon such terms as are customary within the
Programme industry (providing in any event for
minimum limits of cover in the sum of US$1,000,000 for
a single claim and US$3,000,000 for claims in the aggre-
gate and a maximum deductible of US$10,000 for any
one claim) and shall upon demand deliver a copy of the
certificate of insurance to Company B and shall require

Company B, its parent, subsidiaries and related companies to be added as named insureds on such policy which policy shall provide that any monies payable thereunder shall be reimbursed to the party incurring the liability and shall contain an endorsement that negates the "other insurance" clause in the policy and a statement that the insurance being effected is primary and any insurance carried by Company B is neither primary nor contributory.

5. Overspill

Licensor acknowledges that where the Programmes are broadcast by satellite for reception in the Territory, such broadcasts may be capable of reception outside the Territory due to the inherent capability of satellites to beam down signals which are not confined to territorial boundaries ("Overspill"). Licensor further acknowledges that the Rights herein granted to Company B include but are not limited to the right to broadcast the Programmes by satellite that may cause Overspill. Company B agrees that it will scramble its satellite signals of the channels on which a Programme is exhibited and will not knowingly authorise satellite reception by a viewer outside the Territory. Notwithstanding such Overspill, Licensor agrees that the occurrence of Overspill shall not constitute a breach of this Agreement provided that Company B shall have encrypted and not knowingly authorised reception as aforesaid.

6. Indemnity

Licensor shall indemnify and hold harmless Company B in respect of any obligation, claim, action, demand, cost, expense, loss or other liability whatsoever arising directly or indirectly out of or from the exercise of all or any part of the Rights granted to Company B hereunder or any breach of any representation or warranty, agreement or undertaking, whether express or implied, by Licensor hereunder.

7. Taxation and Levies

7.1. Company B is registered for Value Added Tax within the United Kingdom under registration number 440 627467.

7.2.   Licensor warrants that services provided under this Agreement are treated as an Intra-Community supply of Services for Value Added Tax purposes.

7.3.   Licensor undertakes to promptly issue invoices in a form sufficient to enable Company B to fulfil any requirements imposed upon it by any Taxation or Governmental Authority in respect of Value Added Tax. In the event that any Taxation or Governmental Authority carries out an enquiry in respect of the treatment of this Agreement for Value Added Tax purposes then Licensor agrees to promptly and accurately and fully respond to any reasonable request made by Company B to Licensor in respect of such enquiry.

7.4.   If Company B (or any third party authorised by Company B to exercise any of the Rights) is required to pay any fee or levy to any collecting society in connection with the exercise of any of the Rights in respect of any Programme, subject to the proviso in clause 4.5 and save for the Music Performing Rights, then there shall be deducted from the Licence Fee for such Programme an amount equal to any amount so required to be paid. The reduced licence fee resulting from such deduction is referred to as the "Reduced Licence Fee". Company B shall produce to Licensor documentary evidence of any amount which it (or any such third party) has paid to a collecting society in respect of the exercise of any of the Rights, and Licensor shall forthwith repay such amount to Company B, to the extent that the Licence Fee already paid by Company B hereunder exceeds the Reduced Licence Fee.

8. Termination

8.1.   Either party shall be entitled to terminate this Agreement with respect to any one or more of the Programmes forthwith by written notice if the other:

8.1.1.   is in material breach of its warranties or obligations hereunder and such breach is not remedied (if capable of remedy) within thirty (30) days of receipt of written notice specifying the breach and requiring it to be remedied PROVIDED THAT if such material breach relates only to one or more Programmes hereunder the party not in breach shall have the option to terminate this Agreement in its entirety or in respect of such Programme or Programmes and in such an event, this Agreement shall continue in full force and effect in respect of all other Programmes which are not the subject of a material breach as aforesaid; or

8.1.2. goes into receivership or liquidation (other than for the purposes of amalgamation or reconstruction) or becomes insolvent or makes any composition or arrangement with its creditors.

8.2. Company B shall be entitled to terminate this Agreement with respect to a particular Programme or Programmes forthwith by written notice if the BBFC has not awarded such Programme or Programmes a certification of 18 or a less restrictive certification both for theatrical and home video exhibition or, where there is no theatrical exhibition, has not awarded a certification for home video exhibition only.

8.3. Any termination of this Agreement by either party shall be without prejudice to the rights or remedies of either party against the other party in respect of any antecedent breach of the Agreement.

8.4. Without prejudice to any other rights or remedies that either party may have, Licensor acknowledges and agrees that damages may not be an equitable remedy to breach by Licensor of this Agreement and that Company B shall be entitled to the remedies of injunction, specific performance and other equitable relief to any threatened or actual breach of this Agreement by Licensor and that no proof of special damages shall be necessary for the enforcement of these Conditions.

9. Force Majeure

Notwithstanding anything contained in this Agreement if total or partial performance hereof shall be delayed or rendered impossible for either party by virtue of any reason whatsoever beyond its reasonable control (including but not limited to war, invasion, act of foreign enemy hostilities (whether war be declared or not), civil war or strife, rebellion, strikes, lockouts or other industrial disputes or actions, fire, flood, epidemic, earthquake, explosion, decision of any court or other judicial body of competent jurisdiction, transportation, power or satellite failure or non-availability, failure or non-availability of any part of the transmission system whether relating to satellite, cable, terrestrial facilities or other means, acts of God, acts of governments or other prevailing authorities or defaults of third parties) then such non-performance shall not constitute a breach of this Agreement. It is further agreed and understood that if the occurrence of any such event shall prevent Company B from operating any material part of its service then Company B shall so notify Licensor in writing and this Agreement shall be suspended in all respects from the date on which the event of force majeure occurred and shall be resumed with effect from midnight on the day on which the event giving rise to the suspension ceases to the effect that any such period of suspension shall not be included in any calculation of periods of time under this Agreement (other than under the proviso to this clause) PROVIDED ALWAYS that if the Agreement shall be suspended for a consecutive period of twelve (12) months, then at any time thereafter either party may terminate this Agreement forthwith by written notice to the other with respect to the Programme so affected.

10. Rebates

Without prejudice to Company B's rights or remedies for breach of contract, in the event that this Agreement is terminated by either party pursuant to clause 9 or by Company B pursuant to clause 8 in either case with respect to any one or more Programmes, Licensor shall repay to Company B forthwith in respect of each such Programme subject to termination an amount equal to the Licence Fee paid for such Programme less the amount of such Licence Fee attributable to the Exhibition Weeks on which such Programme was exhibited on the Primary Channel prior to such termination.

11. Assignment

11.1.   Neither party hereto shall assign, transfer, charge or make over this Agreement or any of its rights or obligations hereunder except that both Licensor and Company B may assign or sub-license its rights in whole or in part to a "Permitted Transferee". A "Permitted Transferee" shall mean a parent, Subsidiary or Associated Company of Licensor or Company B (as the case may be) or a joint venture to which Company B or Licensor (as the case may be) is a party or a person, firm or corporation who owns or hereafter acquires a substantial portion of Licensor's or Company B's (as the case may be) stock or assets. No transfer shall relieve the transferring party of its obligations hereunder.

11.2.   In the event of an assignment or sub-licence to a Permitted Transferee, the party desiring the assignment or sub-licence must give one month's written notice and the other party agrees to execute and deliver any documents as are requested by the assigning or sub-licensing party as necessary to perfect such assignment or sub-licence.

12. Confidentiality

12.1.   Each party undertakes to the other that, subject to 12.2 below, it shall and shall procure that their respective officers, directors, and employees shall keep confidential the provisions of this Agreement to third parties (other than their agents, representatives, attorneys, professional advisors or to auditors appointed by a distributor of a Programme hereunder who need to know such information as part of its normal reporting or review procedure to its auditors, its shareholders and its parent company ("Distributor Disclosure") save to the extent necessary to enable them to perform their obligations hereunder. The parties shall, and shall procure that such Distributor Disclosure be limited solely with respect to the Programme(s) that require such disclosure and solely to the extent required in order to perform the distribution services contemplated by its agreement with Licensor and shall procure that such Disclosee is bound by the terms of this clause hereunder.

12.2.   Any breach of this clause 12 shall be a material breach of the Agreement save that the provisions of clause 12.1 above shall not apply to any information which:

12.2.1. is in the public domain other than by default of the recipient party;

12.2.2. is obtained by the recipient party from a bona fide third party having no apparent restraint on its free right of disposal of such information; or

12.2.3. is required to be disclosed by law (or applicable regulation) or the valid order or decree of a court of competent jurisdiction by any applicable law, government order or regulation, or the request or direction of any governmental or other regulatory authority or agency.

13. Notice

Any notice given under the provisions under this Agreement shall be in writing and shall be sent to the address of the party to be served as above written or such other address of which notice has previously been given to the other party in accordance with this clause. All notices addressed to Company B shall be marked for the attention of James Conyers, General Counsel. All notices shall be delivered by hand or sent by facsimile (with a copy posted) or, within the United Kingdom, by registered or recorded delivery, or outside the United Kingdom, by registered air mail letter. All notices shall be deemed (until the contrary be proved) to have been received when delivered by hand or on the date on which they would have been received in the normal course of posting (if posted) or if given by facsimile, notices shall be deemed to have been received when transmitted provided that the sender shall have received a transmission report indicating that all pages of the notice have been transmitted to the correct facsimile number.

14. Miscellaneous

14.1. This Agreement represents the entire understanding, and constitutes the entire agreement, in relation to its subject matter and supersedes any previous agreement between the parties with respect thereto and, in particular, excludes any warranty, condition or other undertaking implied by law or by custom. Each party confirms that it has not relied on any representation or warranty or undertaking which is not contained in this Agreement and (without prejudice to any liability for fraudulent misrepresentation) no party shall have any remedy in respect of any misrepresentation or untrue statement made (whether innocently or negligently) by the other party except to the extent (if any) that a claim lies under this Agreement.

14.2. This Agreement may be varied only by an instrument in writing signed on behalf of both parties.

14.3. No failure to exercise nor any delay in exercising any right or remedy hereunder shall operate as a waiver thereof or of any other right or remedy hereunder, nor shall any single or partial exercise of any right or remedy prevent any further or other exercise thereof or the exercise of any other right or remedy. No waiver of any term, provision or condition of this Agreement shall be effective unless it is in writing and signed by the waiving party.

14.4. Nothing in this Agreement is intended to confer any benefit on any third party (whether referred to herein by name, class, description or otherwise) or any right to enforce a term contained in this Agreement.

14.5. The headings in this Agreement have been inserted for convenience only and shall not affect its construction.

14.6. All references in this Agreement to words in the plural form shall be deemed to have been references to the singular where appropriate, and vice versa.

14.7.   There shall survive the expiry or termination of this Agreement any term of this Agreement which in order to give effect its provision needs to survive the said expiry or termination.

14.8.   If any provision of this Agreement should be or become partially or completely ineffective or unenforceable, then such provision shall be struck out but the remaining provisions shall remain unaffected and have full force and effect. In such an event, the parties shall consult with a view to negotiating in good faith an alternative provision which substantially gives effect to the parties' intentions at the date hereof and which no longer is ineffective or unenforceable. In the event that, within sixty (60) days of the commencement of discussions, no such mutually satisfactory agreement can be reached which in the opinion of the parties substantially gives effect to their respective original intentions and which is effective and enforceable, then, subject to clause 14.9 below, either Company B or Licensor may at any time thereafter terminate this Agreement by written notice to the other party provided that the other party shall not be deemed to have waived its right to terminate hereunder as a result of not exercising such right before the other party.

14.9.   The right of termination of the parties set out in clause 14.8 above shall be used in good faith and only where the commercial benefit of this Agreement for the party exercising such right of termination has in practice been diminished in consequence of such provision becoming partially or completely ineffective or unenforceable.

14.10. This Agreement shall be governed by and interpreted in accordance with the laws of England and the parties agree to submit to the exclusive jurisdiction of the English Courts as regards any claim or matter arising in relation hereto.

Index